ANNA HICKEY-MOODY, SOPHIE HARTLEY, PETER KELLY, TAMMY WONG HULBERT, SCOTT BROOK, RIMI KHAN AND CHRISTEN CORNELL

YOUTH ARTS

Creative Production and Skills for Work

POLICY PRESS SHORTS RESEARCH

First published in Great Britain in 2026 by

Policy Press, an imprint of
Bristol University Press
University of Bristol
1–9 Old Park Hill
Bristol
BS2 8BB
UK
t: +44 (0)117 374 6645
e: bup-info@bristol.ac.uk

Details of international sales and distribution partners are available at
policy.bristoluniversitypress.co.uk

DOI: 10.51952/9781447379270

British Library Cataloguing in Publication Data
A catalogue record for this book is available from the British Library

ISBN 978-1-4473-7925-6 paperback
ISBN 978-1-4473-7926-3 ePub
ISBN 978-1-4473-7927-0 OA PDF

Cover design: Kitty Russell
Front cover image: Shutterstock/Melinda Nagy
Bristol University Press and Policy Press use environmentally responsible print partners.
Printed and bound in Great Britain by CPI Group (UK) Ltd, Croydon, CR0 4YY

Bristol University Press' authorised representative in the European Union is: Easy Access System Europe, Mustamäe tee 50, 10621 Tallinn, Estonia,
Email: gpsr.requests@easproject.com

FSC
www.fsc.org
MIX
Paper | Supporting responsible forestry
FSC® C013604

Contents

About the authors		iv
Acknowledgements		v
Preface		vii
one	Introduction	1
PART I	**Reimagining the problem of youth**	
two	Reframing youth agency	21
three	The futures of skills, work and credentialing	35
PART II	**The creative industries: partnerships, practices, diverse economies**	
four	Promising partnerships and technology futures	67
five	Practices	88
six	Diverse economies	112
seven	Conclusion	137
Notes		166
References		167
Index		184

About the authors

Scott Brook is Associate Professor of Communication at the Royal Melbourne Institute of Technology (RMIT) University.

Christen Cornell is Research Fellow and Manager of Research Partnerships at Creative Australia.

Sophie Hartley is Research Associate at Deakin University and Researcher at the Commons Social Change Library.

Anna Hickey-Moody is Director of the Arts and Humanities Institute at Maynooth University and inaugural Senior Academic Leadership Ireland Professor of Intersectional Humanities.

Tammy Wong Hulbert is an artist and curator, and Senior Lecturer at the RMIT University School of Art.

Peter Kelly is Professor of Education at Deakin University.

Rimi Khan is Associate Professor of Fashion and RMIT Vice Chancellor's Research Fellow at RMIT Melbourne.

Acknowledgements

This book emerges from the Vital Arts research project, hosted at RMIT University, which has been made possible through the collaboration, creativity and generosity of many people and organisations. We would like to extend our heartfelt thanks to our industry partners, whose vision and commitment to inclusive, experimental and transformative arts practices shaped the project from its earliest stages.

The project was funded by the Australian Research Council's (ARC) Industry Linkage Project Scheme as project LP200301027 Creative industries pathways to youth employment in the COVID-19 recession and co-funded both in cash and in kind by our key industry partners, Creative Australia, The Push Pty Ltd, Australian Theatre for Young People (ATYP), Centre for Multicultural Youth (CMY) and Future Foundations. Without financial investment from these companies, and considerable in-kind support in the form of expertise and engagement, this project would not have been possible. We extend genuine appreciation and thanks. Non-financial partners who supported this work include Back to Back Theatre, Carclew Youth Arts Centre, L2R Dance and Gippsland Art Gallery. We gratefully acknowledge the contributions of our partners across the arts, education and community sectors, including those who have provided feedback, opened rehearsal rooms, welcomed research participants and tested pilot versions of our micro-credentials and training materials. Each organisation and individual has played a vital role in ensuring that the materials we develop remain grounded in real-world practice, accessible to diverse learners and responsive to the needs of the sector.

We would also like to acknowledge the generous support of Professor Lisa French, Dean of the School of Media and Communication at RMIT University, who supported the continuation and completion of this work, and Professor Tim Marshall, Deputy Vice Chancellor of Design and Social Context at RMIT. Thanks also to Denise Stanley from CLOCK Your Skills, Deakin University's School of Education and the Maynooth University Arts and Humanities Institute, Ireland.

Preface

Hannah hated high school in small, quiet ways that really added up. The long walk up the school driveway created a sinking feeling in her stomach and a rising tightness in her chest. The dread really was not worth it. The constricting in her chest when she saw groups huddled at lockers made her feel like she couldn't breathe. The ways conversations dipped when she walked past: the new girl. The flicker of another student's eyes that seemed to say, 'what's wrong with you?' She never knew how to explain what was wrong, because everything was falling apart. You can't put that in words.

At home, Hannah moved through the mornings with dread. The kettle whistling. The smell of toast that was just beginning to burn because she was helping Dad button his shirt. His fingers didn't listen to him anymore. 'Leave it', he'd mutter, embarrassed. 'It's fine', she'd say, doing up each button. One. Two. Three. She knew the schedule of his carer's visits better than she knew her school timetable. She knew which days were bad, and more and more he couldn't get out of bed. The house always felt thick with something unspoken. The rising panic of his illness silently creeping through their life. By the time she reached school, Hannah felt like she had already lived a full day. And still, she was expected to sit still. To listen. To care about quizzes and lunchtime gossip. Every molecule of her being wanted to run away. She felt like a ghost moving through fluorescent corridors. The teachers thought she was distant. Moody. Anti-social. They didn't see the exhaustion tucked beneath her ribs. The constant low hum of worry. Most days, as the bell rang for third period, something inside her would snap. A quiet, decisive no. Instead of turning towards the school block, she'd slip down through the dry creek running out the back of the school, heart racing, not with rebellion, but relief. The bus, the traffic, city air felt wider. Kinder. She was anonymous and free with no responsibility for a few hours.

There was an abandoned building near the edge of town, cracked brick and shattered windows. The roof sagged like it was tired. Weeds clawed their way through the pavement. No one went there. Which meant it belonged to Hannah on her afternoons in town.

Hannah would drag her paint-splattered backpack inside, dust swirling in beams of light that fell through broken panes. The air smelled of rust and damp concrete. At first, her hands would tremble, from fear of being caught, from the leftover tension of school, but the moment the colour touched the wall, something in her chest loosened. She painted girls with ribcages being turned into violins, becoming swans, riding away dressed as men: stories from her father's songs. She made murals of doors swinging open. She painted fathers made of glass, light shining through their many cracks. She painted enormous skies breaking through ceilings. The brush against the brick was steady. Certain. She didn't feel judged. Her feelings had somewhere to go. Anger became thick, red strokes. Fear became thin blue lines threading through everything. When she painted, she wasn't the strange girl. She wasn't the carer. She wasn't the one who left early. She was just ... Alive.

The day she was discovered, Hannah's stomach dropped so hard she thought she might faint.

She had been halfway up a shaky ladder, adding delicate white cracks to the wings of a painted figure, when she heard heels clicking against concrete. Sharp. Measured. Unmistakable. She turned. Standing in the doorway was Ms Devereaux. Her drama teacher. She looked wildly out of place among the rubble. Ms Devereaux always appeared like a cartoon character: sharp lines, leather skirt, crisp blouse, pencil-thin eyebrows arched like careful brushstrokes, red lipstick so precise it seemed drawn on with a ruler. Not a hair out of place. Her eyes moved slowly over the mural. Up. Across. Taking in every detail. Hannah's mouth went dry.

She imagined the phone call home. The disappointment. The word truancy stamped across her record like a bruise. Again. Another school that was going to ask her to leave. Instead, Ms Devereaux tilted her head. 'Well', she said coolly, folding her arms. 'That explains a great deal.' Hannah climbed down, pulse roaring in her ears. Ms Devereaux stepped closer to the wall. Her red lips curved not into a smile exactly, but something softer. 'You have great potential, Hannah', she said quietly. 'And you've had nowhere to put it.' Hannah stared at the cracked floor. Ms Devereaux glanced around the ruined building. 'This', she said, gesturing at the mural, 'is not vandalism. It's vision. Though I would strongly prefer it not involve skipping my classes.' Despite herself, Hannah let out a shaky breath of something almost like a laugh.

'We're staging *The Importance of Being Earnest* for the Year 12 major production', Ms Devereaux continued. 'I need a stage designer. Someone who understands what sits beneath polite surfaces.' Her pencil-thin eyebrows lifted. 'You, Hannah, understand that very well.'

The theatre was not that different from the warehouse. It was dusty, and dark, and quiet, but intentional. The stage was empty and expectant, not abandoned. The curtains were deep burgundy velvet, heavy, dusty and dramatic. Lights hung overhead like watchful stars. At first, Hannah hovered at the edges. The cast were loud, confident, attractive, brimming with insider jokes. Of course they were. She felt the old tightness return, that familiar sense of being slightly out of focus in everyone else's world. But then she stood alone on the stage one afternoon, script in hand, and read the play properly. *The Importance of Being Earnest* was a comedy, but beneath the wit was something sharp. Everyone is pretending. Everyone is performing versions of themselves. Double names. Double lives. Hannah understood that intimately. She designed tall, elegant Victorian panels, cream and gold with peacocks, and she made them slightly distorted. The doorframes leaned just a fraction. The painted wallpaper patterns didn't quite align. Perfection unsettled. Behind each pristine wall, she painted hidden layers: wild gardens clawing upward, cracks splitting porcelain surfaces, constellations bleeding through polite drawing rooms. During rehearsals, while actors delivered clever lines, Hannah painted in silence under warm stage lights. Her fingers were smudged with colour. Her cheeks streaked with accidental gold. People came to her with questions. 'Does this look right?' 'Where should I stand?' 'Can we move this piece?' The tightness in her chest began to ease. Her creativity, once squeezed into stolen afternoons, was expanding. It stretched across flats and backdrops, climbed ladders, spilled into lighting discussions. It had space. In the years that followed, Hannah would always remember that creativity saved her not by changing her life, but by giving her a space big enough for her heart to breathe.

Hannah is a character based on a real person and real life experiences. Stories of young lives are woven through this book as narratives that are based on our research. We do this in order to bring young people's experiences into the heart of this work. Youth agency is a key theme in this book. We write for youth workers, educators, creative industries professionals: for people who work with young people who can't stop moving, who like making things, who answer back and question. This book is for the rare adults who care about the kids that spend afternoons sketching in the margins of exercise books, rearranging sounds into songs or moving their bodies into rhythms that don't fit the school bell. We see you.

Growing up as a creative child often means learning that your ways of knowing and doing are not recognised. The school classroom rewards rote learning, neat handwriting and 'the right answers' more than the ability to imagine otherwise, to do and to question. The school yard can feel like a place where creativity is eccentric at best, suspect at worst. The world of exams, test scores and classroom noise rarely makes space for the quiet determination of kids who need to tinker, shape, perform and invent.

Creativity is a form of intelligence (Kim et al, 2010). It is resilience, problem solving and generates joy. It is the way that communities survive, how stories endure and how cultures grow (Gunnestad, 2006). Creativity is also a way of making sense of who we are, especially when the world around us is often confusing, heavy or unjust.

This book is written in recognition of the young people whose gifts were overlooked, dismissed or undervalued at school, not because they lacked talent or persistence but because the systems around them didn't yet know how to measure what they had to offer. It is also a celebration: of imagination, of doing things differently, making it against the odds and of the value that comes from following the impulse to create, even when nobody is watching.

To every youth worker who makes space and time for young people who like doing and making: *your skills matter*. Your ideas matter. Your work changes the world in ways that numbers can't capture. May this book remind us all that being creative is not a side-note to life but one of its most profound expressions.

ONE

Introduction

Young people are known for their curiosity, rebellion and energy: in fact, research has been attempting to describe, problematise and even shape young people for decades (Kelly, 2000; Moje, 2002). Young people attract the attention of scholars across education, sociology, psychology, marketing, risk management, technology development, and this list could go on. Ideologies of every stripe look to the future and argue that it contains young people, transferable skills, flexible workforces and the digital. So, we know what these key ingredients for the future of work are, *but what should we do with this information? How can we employ it to support young people?*

As recent scholarship has identified, years of uncertainty about youth employability, exacerbated by the Global Financial Crisis (GFC) of 2008 and the COVID-19 pandemic, have regularly been met with individualising discourses that position young people as fundamentally *lacking*: in skills, networks, opportunities (Leonard and Wilde, 2019). Thus various programmes, interventions and policies are proposed to fill the gaps in young people themselves. In contrast, this book asks readers to re-think the politics of scholarship on youth, turning these discourses of deficit on their head. Grounded in practice-based research with youth arts organisations, this work demonstrates that skills are not a matter of *have* or *have not* but are always in motion, in a state of becoming within young people. Our ethnographic fieldwork with youth arts programmes shows young people already engaging in the very skills demanded for the future of work: critical thinking, creativity, collaboration and curiosity. The issue then becomes not how to *give* young people the skills they *lack* to secure employment but instead how our contemporary education and labour markets can effectively capture, acknowledge and accredit skills as they already exist in motion in young people.

We build on work undertaken in an action research project – Vital Arts: Skilling Young People for their Futures, which was co-funded by arts industry partners and government. We designed and implemented a model for accrediting the practical skills that young people develop through youth arts education. The research team conducted extensive fieldwork with young people in arts and cultural diversity-focused organisations to assess their skills, learning needs and experiences. As a result of this fieldwork, Vital Arts partnered with UK-based organisation CLOCK Your Skills, and we worked together to develop a series of micro-credentials that can be run with youth arts organisations to accredit 21st-century skills. This not only provides an accreditation for young people to support future study and employment but demonstrates the value of the youth arts sector as a forum for skills development (Montgomery, 2017; Campbell, 2019).

Vital Arts is built on the World Economic Forum's (WEF, 2016) identification of the 21st-century skills that it and other government, business and international organisations have indicated young people need to develop to participate actively in new worlds of work. The project created new ways of valuing practice-based learning for young people in the creative industries, and, based on this valuation, this book builds pathways into scholarship and academic work in the creative industries that are designed likewise to value practice-based learning. Such mechanisms for recognising skills are vital if we are going to diversify the workforce of the creative sector.

We offer a fresh engagement with youth studies scholarship. The term 'young people' combines hopes and anxieties; it's a euphemism for possibility and can be a metonym for diverse ideologies. The paradoxical appeal of older people writing about troubled youth has been unshakeable since the post-war 'TV generation' who enjoyed newly won disposable incomes and the introduction of 'youth music' on the radio, making teens a consumer category (Hall and Jefferson, 2006; Laughey, 2006; Meaney, 2020). Intervening in this landscape from a critical and constructive perspective, we ask how youth arts, skills, work and arts education in globalised and globalising contexts position the teen as both consumer and worker. Through offering new models for recognising informal education and the development of 21st-century skills, Vital Arts also reframes micro-credentials as a method for inclusive education and a pathway into higher education for students who might not be achieving within school contexts. In developing these discussions, we draw on interdisciplinary and diverse sources from within and outside academia. Our work is informed by youth voices and energies. We are also influenced by youth popular culture, although we are broadly critical of the capitalist overcoding that redistributes young people's cultural capital for capitalist gain.

Youth arts industries and cultures

As our fieldwork demonstrates, youth arts are a dynamic and evolving sector that provide young people with opportunities for developing skills and participating in community engagement. Across Australia and Europe, youth arts organisations operate in diverse contexts, from urban cultural hubs to regional and rural communities. These spaces offer informal education, complementing or challenging traditional school-based learning. Unlike formal education, youth arts programmes centre youth voice and agency. They work through co-creation, youth-led initiatives and collaborative practice, affording young people a level of ownership that is often absent from structured educational settings. This is one of the reasons why the youth arts context is so valuable. It requires young people to stand up, speak up, take advice on board and then make it work.

As the then artistic director of a major Australian youth arts organisation described during our research interviews, the attitude of 'mutual respect' between youth arts facilitators and the young people they work with allows these programmes to cultivate transferable skills in a non-hierarchical environment: '[I]t really is generally an attitude of mutual respect in that context that we don't often see in an educational context' (Fraser Corfield, ATYP).

While traditional school settings often prioritise standardised testing and curriculum-driven outcomes, youth arts programmes focus on experiential learning, problem solving and social-emotional development. Work can be quite unique to the individual. Participants in youth arts initiatives often gain embodied confidence in public speaking, teamwork, leadership and self-expression: skills that are valuable both within and beyond the arts sector. For example, theatre-based youth programmes in Australia, such as those facilitated by organisations like ATYP, encourage young people to write, direct and perform their own work. In the Northern Territory, Corrugated Iron Youth Arts' 'Champions' programme allows young people to be actively involved in governance, decision making and planning programmes at the organisation. These experiences develop critical thinking and communication skills while also empowering participants to shape narratives that matter to them.

In Europe, youth arts organisations such as Contact Theatre in the UK and Youth Theatre Ireland provide platforms where young people actively engage in devising performances, making artistic decisions and influencing the direction of creative projects. These settings contrast sharply with traditional readings of young people as passive recipients of civic education (Harris, 2017). In the youth arts programmes we witnessed, young people are recognised as cultural producers, capable of shaping artistic and social discourse. Fraser Corfield of ATYP described the ways that youth arts can cultivate civic and cultural literacy: '[Y]oung people that participate in the arts and participate in the performing arts in particular are far more likely to vote, they're more likely to volunteer for community organisations, they're more likely to get involved in civic activity' (Fraser Corfield, ATYP).

Research backs this up, with various studies finding that participation in youth arts can boost civic engagement, particularly for marginalised young people (Catterall, 2009; Catterall et al, 2012). Taken as a model, youth arts processes foster a sense of autonomy and investment, encouraging participants to see themselves as active agents in both their creative and social worlds. In this sense, the youth arts context can be seen as an ideal way to cultivate brave and adaptable workers for the new world of work.

Youth arts also play a crucial role in fostering intercultural dialogue and social inclusion. Many initiatives explicitly engage with marginalised communities, offering young people from diverse backgrounds a space to explore identity, belonging and political agency through artistic practice. For instance, arts-based youth programmes in refugee communities across Europe use storytelling and digital media to help young people articulate their experiences and perspectives (Lenette, 2019; Boukhari, 2025). In Australia, organisations such as Big hART, RANT Arts and Corrugated Iron Youth Arts work with young people in remote and disadvantaged communities, providing platforms where their voices and experiences can be amplified through music, visual art and performance.

The informal learning that occurs within youth arts settings is often more adaptable and responsive to individual needs than traditional schooling, where pressures of league tables and educational markets can lead to inequities of student support and outcomes (Cieslik and Simpson, 2017; McLaughlin, 2024). Programmes frequently employ participatory and experimental pedagogies, allowing young people to learn through doing, failing and experimenting in a supportive environment. Programme leaders that were interviewed for the research spoke about how the concept of play was integral to youth arts, creating an environment where failure was not final but an opportunity for curiosity, exploration and learning. Young people were 'allowed to fail' in these contexts without fear of getting left behind (interview participant).

Peer-to-peer relationships are central to how these pedagogies work and tend to build morale while also developing critical faculties. This fosters intrinsic motivation, as young people engage with artistic challenges that are meaningful to them rather than externally imposed. In this respect, youth arts can offer a much-needed counterpoint to formal education, providing young people with agency, creative autonomy and the opportunity to develop skills in self-directed ways. Across Australia and Europe, youth arts organisations not only shape the cultural landscape but also nurture the next generation of creative, critical and socially engaged citizens (Burgess et al, 2006; De Roeper and Savelsberg, 2009).

Youth agency and the 'wildness' of youth

We are interested in what we call the 'wildness' of youth: agency as it might be expressed in between structure and embodied capacities to act. In the literature (Threadgold et al, 2021; Ivinson and Renold, 2022), there is a continued recognition of youth agency as a dynamic and multifaceted construct. Scholars emphasise that youth agency is influenced by various factors, including individual capacities (Halberstam, 2020), social contexts (Coffey and Farrugia, 2013) and structural constraints (Hunter, 2020).

Outside youth studies as a field, researchers have employed theoretical frameworks such as social-ecological models (Darling, 2007), capability approaches (Nussbam, 2000; McDonald et al, 2010: 140) and intersectionality (Phoenix and Pattynama, 2006) to understand the interplay between individual agency and broader socio-cultural factors. When these concerns are brought into a youth context, there are a range of contextual factors that shape youth agency and need to be considered. These include family dynamics, peer relationships, school environments and community structures. As one might imagine, the research cited earlier indicates that supportive relationships, positive role models and access to resources enhance youth agency, while adverse conditions such as poverty, discrimination and violence can limit it.

With the rapid advancement of digital technologies, literature has explored the role of technology in fostering youth agency (Goldman et al, 2008; Ringrose et al, 2024). Studies highlight how young people use digital platforms, social media and online communities to express themselves, engage in civic activities and mobilise for social change (Hickey-Moody and Willcox, 2025). Digital spaces provide new avenues for youth participation, allowing young individuals to amplify their voices and challenge traditional power structures (Vromen, 2008). Micro-credentials and digital open badges are part of the broader digital infrastructure that scaffolds youth engagement with education in the contemporary moment. The way young people engage with education and skills development in a rapidly evolving digital landscape is changing all the time and will continue to be fluid. As young people increasingly participate in digital cultures, through social media, gaming, online content creation and collaborative platforms, digital badges offer a means to formalise and extend the skills they are already developing informally (see McGillivray et al, 2016). This intersection between digital cultures and learning captured in the digital badge is reshaping how young people access, apply and capitalise on their knowledge in the workforce.

Young people navigate highly interactive and participatory digital environments. They create and curate content on platforms like YouTube, TikTok and Instagram (Bermúdez, 2023; Márquez et al, 2023). They collaborate on projects via Discord and Slack; engage in digital storytelling through gaming and streaming; and develop technical skills in coding, graphic design and video editing. For many young people, these skills are acquired informally, through self-directed learning, peer networks and online tutorials.

While schools may teach digital literacy, they cannot account for the complexity and innovation happening in young people's digital spaces (Bulfin and North, 2007). Traditional education systems are increasingly turning to micro-credentials as ways of facilitating a focus on areas of skill development that are not part of core school curriculum areas. One of our interviewees, who is the head of education at a major Australian cultural organisation, saw the potential for micro-credentials to 'change pedagogy' and 'get teachers thinking about different ways of doing things'. For this interviewee, this meant more project-based learning and giving students the opportunity to participate in creative programmes outside the school setting. Our research has found that micro-credentials can bridge this gap by providing structured, industry-recognised certification for skills that are already being cultivated outside formal education.

> Shay always arrived before the bands did. They liked the dark and the quiet of the Brunswick studio before the amps hummed awake and the tramlines outside began to sing with drunk passengers. Non-binary, sharp-eared and softly spoken, Shay had become the go-to sound designer for a handful of high-profile local Melbourne bands: acts who could sell out rooms in Collingwood and Northcote without much radio play, carried mostly by word of mouth and Shay's immaculate live mixes.
>
> At the back of the venue, laptop open, Shay moved between programs with the ease of someone switching instruments.

A session in Abbotsford. A shared folder of stems in the cloud. A Discord server pinging gently in the corner of the screen. For Shay, sound wasn't just frequencies and faders; it was workflow, communication, infrastructure. It was knowing how to build a digital ecosystem where guitarists uploaded demos on time, drummers labelled their takes properly and no one lost the final mix in a maze of 'FINAL_v3_REALFINAL.wav'.

The bands loved that about them. Rehearsals ran more smoothly. Remote collaborations actually happened. Touring musicians could check mixes from hotel rooms in Sydney or Berlin, leaving timestamped notes in a Discord channel Shay had set up with neat little threads: #drum-edits, #vocal-takes, #merch-audio, #random-2am-ideas. What used to dissolve into chaos now felt like a collective practice.

It was this quiet mastery that caught the attention of their TAFE teacher,[1] Greg, who still wore bootcut jeans and carried a USB stick on a lanyard. Without irony. Greg had taught Shay the basics of signal flow and microphone placement years ago. But the curriculum hadn't changed much since then. 'Can I show you something?' Shay dropped in to see him one afternoon, sitting beside him in the half-lit computer lab, enjoying the air conditioning.

They walked him through Discord, not as a gaming chat app but as a production hub. They showed him how channels could mirror the stages of a sound project, how bots could automate file backups, how students could critique mixes asynchronously. They mapped out a new module: collaborative online production, version control, digital etiquette, remote mixing workflows. Shay suggested integrating current DAWs,[2] cloud-based mastering tools, even a unit on building an online presence as a sound designer in Melbourne's live scene. Greg listened, at first wary, then slowly grinning.

By the next semester, the course outline had changed. Students built servers instead of just studio sessions. They learned how to manage creative teams across time zones, how to name files properly, how to give feedback that was precise and kind. Shay came in as a guest teacher, standing at the front of the same room where they'd once sat, explaining gain staging and group chat moderation with equal seriousness.

In the studio that night, as a bassline bloomed warm and clean through the speakers, Shay felt the quiet satisfaction of a well-balanced mix. Not just frequencies aligned, but generations. Old knowledge and new tools. Analog and digital. Teacher and student.

In tune.

This vignette, and the young people who taught us about these critical skills for industry work, show how the rise of automation, artificial intelligence and digital transformation in the workforce has increased the demand for adaptable, tech-savvy professionals (Berown et al, 2022). Employers in the creative industries need workers who possess a blend of technical expertise, problem-solving abilities and creativity: skills that are nurtured in digital environments but not necessarily validated through traditional degrees.

Educational privilege and traditional curricula reproduce inequities in future employment. Privileged students can interiorise social class divisions as 'moral differentiations' through discourses of meritocracy (Uboldi, 2024). Class inequities apparent in creative professions are thus cultivated in earlier educational contexts (Uboldi, 2024). To put this another way, employers often struggle to recruit the kinds of workers they need because private schools and traditional curricula tend to produce young people who expect to be carefully instructed rather than workers with radical agency and a brave attitude. Class privilege creates a workforce that reproduces, rather than challenges, the contemporary global landscape of disaster, instability and mistrust (Beck, 2000).

One of the key strengths of micro-credentials is their accessibility. They are often low cost, they can be available online and designed for self-paced learning. This flexibility allows young people to integrate learning into their daily lives, complementing their existing digital engagement. Moreover, micro-credentials often involve project-based learning, where participants apply skills in real-world contexts, aligning with the experiential, hands-on nature of youth digital cultures. Unlike traditional schooling, which follows rigid curricula, micro-credential programmes allow learners to tailor their skill development to their interests and career aspirations. For example, a young person interested in gaming can earn credentials in game development or e-sports management, building on their existing expertise. Micro-credentials offer a bridge between the digital cultures of young people and the growing need for additional skills development. By providing flexible, accessible and industry-relevant learning opportunities, they validate and extend the informal learning that occurs in digital spaces. As the workforce continues to evolve, micro-credentials already play an increasingly crucial role in ensuring that young people remain empowered, skilled and future ready. Many large corporations, such as Deloitte, Amazon and LinkedIn, now build teams and manage project staffing through in-house micro-credentials that are awarded by management teams and are relied upon to demonstrate skill sets.

These themes of intersectionality, digital skills, youth agency and microcreds as equity pathways are the main ingredients for the study that informs this book. We start with young people, agency, arts practice and the possibility that micro-credentials can be employed to recognise the valuable learning that young people undertake in youth arts contexts. What if young people graduated from youth arts programmes with an accreditation of the skills they had learnt and demonstrated? What if there were pathways into the workforce from this point? These were the questions that prompted the Vital Arts project, which between 2022 and 2026 worked closely with industry to assess the extent to which youth arts programmes might actually prepare young people for a diverse world of work that extends beyond, but also includes, the creative industries.

Vital Arts

As part of the Vital Arts project, we completed a comprehensive policy, literature and product analysis of micro-credentials available in Australia (Hickey-Moody et al, 2025). Through the research process, we have identified key barriers to inclusion within these short courses. These include financial barriers: while it is possible to design low-cost, accessible micro-credentials, many existing micro-credentials are costly, especially for individuals from lower socio-economic backgrounds, which limits accessibility to those who can afford them. Geographic and technology-related barriers are also significant, particularly in remote and rural regions, as limited access to high-speed internet can restrict learners' ability to engage in online learning opportunities. Further, many micro-credentials rely heavily on access to digital infrastructure, excluding learners without regular access to computers. Existing micro-credentials cater to narrow online learning models, which may not suit diverse learners, particularly those who benefit from the more practical, hands-on approaches that are familiar in youth arts contexts.

To address these challenges, the Vital Arts project has focused on practical skills recognition. While we found the previously mentioned shortcomings in many of the existing micro-credentials on the market, the value of micro-credentials is in their adaptability, and we thus set about to design micro-credentials that could be more accessible, adaptable and valuable to young people. We partnered with CLOCK Your Skills, who specialise in developing short courses that make invisible skills visible and valuable (CLOCK Your Skills, 2025). Through this partnership, we engaged in a collaborative co-design process to develop Australia's first truly accessible micro-credentials.

This partnership aims to overcome the barriers identified earlier by creating a micro-credential that is more affordable, provides an accessible workshop-style learning model, with in-person options, and works effectively in the hands-on youth arts-based context. The Vital Arts collaboration with CLOCK Your Skills allowed us to create the first micro-credentials that accredit the real-world skills that young people develop through participation in youth arts programmes. Our research methods were framed within action research cycles and included ethnographic observation, interview and policy analysis. These three forms of data collection occurred iteratively across the youth arts organisations with whom we collaborated.

Intersectionality

> Mai always chose a seat slightly off-centre. Not hidden exactly, but not claiming the middle either. From there, she could see everyone: who leaned forward when they spoke, who performed with ease, who kept checking their phone screen when they thought no one noticed. The workshop was being held on the main stage of the company's flagship theatre in Sydney. The house lights were up, exposing the red velvet seats and the faint scuff marks along the aisles. It felt strange to be so visible in a space usually devoted to illusion. The stage smelled of dust and warm metal, like old rigging and new ambition.
>
> Mai tucked her hair behind her ear and listened. She was small, but not fragile. There was something tensile about her: like a wire pulled tight. She wore black jeans and a faded T-shirt from a student production she had stage managed years ago. When she smiled, which she did often, it was quick and contained, as though she were careful about how much space even her happiness took up.
>
> 'What skills do you need to make it in the creative industries?' the facilitator asked.

The answers came easily from the group:

- resilience
- networking
- self-producing
- grant writing
- adaptability

Mai nodded at each one. She had all of them, or was trying to learn them. She had worked front-of-house shifts between rehearsals. She had rewritten grant applications for friends at midnight. She knew how to make herself useful in a rehearsal room.

When it was her turn, she spoke clearly but without flourish. 'Understanding the ecosystem', she said. 'Knowing where your work fits.' It sounded strategic. Mature. It was also a quiet confession. Conversations continued on. In the middle of the to and fro, the lights cut out mid-discussion.

A clean mechanical click, and then darkness. The timer. No override. A few startled laughs fluttered across the stage before dissolving into a thick, enveloping black. The theatre dark was complete: no ambient glow, no spill from the foyer. Just breath and space.

In that darkness, Mai felt her shoulders drop. She could exhale fully.

Without faces turned towards her, without the subtle calibrations of eye contact, she could speak from somewhere less guarded.

'I completely rewrote my play', she said into the darkness.

Her voice carried effortlessly into the auditorium. The acoustics held her gently, amplified but not exposed.

'The first version had three Asian girls', she continued. 'They were specific. They had specific families. Specific jokes. It was set where I grew up.'

She could see it even now: the fluorescent-lit kitchen, the rice cooker clicking off, the girls switching between English and Mandarin mid-sentence. It had been funny. Sharp. Alive.

'I changed them', she said simply. 'Because I knew it wouldn't get cast.'

The dark theatre was silent, though not empty.

'There aren't enough Asian actors coming through youth theatre here. Not enough to build a full cast without it being seen as ... niche.' She chose the word carefully. 'So I made the characters less culturally fixed. I took out details. Made it more open.'

More universal, she almost said. But she didn't. 'That's the version that got me into this programme.' The silence that followed was different from before. It wasn't awkward. But it was heavy with recognition. Mai wasn't angry. She wasn't even accusing. She was precise.

She had done the maths. She had traced the pathway: school drama programmes with limited diversity; youth ensembles that rarely reflected the suburbs she knew; drama schools drawing from those same pipelines; mainstage companies claiming they couldn't cast what they couldn't see. She understood that representation on stage was only the visible tip of a much longer structure. So she had adjusted her script to fit the structure.

In the dark, she named the skill she had never seen listed on a funding form: anticipatory self-editing. The capacity to bend before being told to. The instinct to remove friction so the work could move forward. The lights snapped back on. For a second, everyone blinked against the brightness. The red seats re-emerged. The circle of chairs felt smaller.

Mai looked the same. She is calm, composed, hands resting lightly on her knees, but something had shifted around her. The conversation about resilience now felt insufficient.

> Adaptability sounded different in the air. She had not asked for sympathy. She had offered data. Lived data.
>
> In centring her story, the absence became visible: the missing intersectional pathways in youth arts. The gap between diversity rhetoric and sustained training. The way institutions often celebrate 'new voices' without ensuring the conditions for those voices to remain intact. Mai sat back slightly, no longer off-centre but unmistakably central. The stage, which had seemed so vast and impersonal at the beginning of the workshop, now felt like a listening body. And for once, she had not rewritten herself to fit it.

Scholars have paid increasing attention to the intersectionality of youth agency, recognising that young people experience multiple forms of marginalisation based on race, gender, sexuality and class (Rodó-de-Zárate, 2017; von Benzon and Wilkinson, 2019; Robinson and Schmitz, 2021). They emphasise the importance of considering the unique experiences of marginalised youth and understanding how intersecting identities can both enhance and constrain agency. Intersectional approaches highlight the need for inclusive and equitable policies and interventions. Taking an intersectional approach to research, Vital Arts builds on studies that have explored the implications of youth agency for policy development and implementation. The micro-credentials we built capture and represent the transferable skills that diverse young people develop in varied contexts. Our project design recognises the significance of this diversity in the expertise and perspectives of young people, and we advocate for participatory approaches that involve youth in decision making. Youth-led initiatives, youth councils and youth advisory boards are some examples of the mechanisms that our project consulted, employed and celebrated to foster youth agency and empower young individuals as agents of change. Our project engages with these mechanisms in our partner organisations and also includes the voices of diverse young people through fieldwork observation, paid focus groups, interviews and a survey. This approach ensures that the skills and competencies recognised through the programme are accessible to all participants, especially those with low socio-economic status, non-English-speaking backgrounds or marginalised identities. Through collaboration with a diverse range of partners, Vital Arts is committed to fostering equitable opportunities and acknowledging the multifaceted identities of youth in the arts sector.

The structure of this book

This book is in two parts. The first half focuses on youth studies scholarship and recent research on the future of work. The opening chapter introduces problems with how youth and work have been conceived, setting the stage for the rest of our analysis. Subsequent chapters in the first section examine youth governance, the economic precarity of young people living in late-stage capitalism and the ways in which policy discourses frame their futures. These discussions engage with key concepts such as intersectionality, class, gender, race and the neoliberal restructuring of work.

The second half of the book turns to examine the creative industries and the material-creative ecosystems that house our creds. We examine how contemporary social, economic and political forces shape the lives of young people, particularly in relation to employment, education and skills development. We situate young people within broader discourses of problematisation: both in terms of how young people are framed as social problems and how they experience challenges within the rapidly evolving labour market. The second half of the book also offers examples of how young people develop transferable skills through participation in arts-based education and creative industries, and how these skills can be recognised, accredited and valued. The discussion is grounded in our case studies of youth arts organisations and their role in fostering skills development outside traditional educational frameworks. We introduce key concepts related to the creative industries, including partnerships, practices and diverse economies. We place significant focus on micro-credentialing as a mechanism for recognising and legitimising transferable skills within broader employment contexts.

The concluding chapter synthesises the book's arguments, reflecting on how young people's creative work and participation in the arts can challenge dominant narratives about skills, employment and social value. This calls for a rethinking of how youth work is conceptualised, advocating for policies and practices that recognise and support diverse forms of knowledge and expertise. The significance of this book lies in its intervention in ongoing debates about youth, work and the creative economy. By linking youth studies with research on creative labour, we provide a fresh perspective on how young people navigate and reimagine their futures.

PART I

Reimagining the problem of youth

TWO

Reframing youth agency

The field of youth studies, broadly defined, began as a way of exploring concerns with problem youth, as in young people who cause trouble at school or in society, and also as a way of better understanding the problems that young people face. Some of these social and economic problems are enduring and relate to broader issues such as intersectionality, class, gender, race, disability and so on. However, contemporary technologies, workshop spaces, generational mindsets and attitudes have changed and shape challenges that young people need to negotiate. A number of scholarly projects have critically engaged with the fact that policy discourses and associated funding models not only rely on young people's problems and young people being a problem but also 're-make' the issues they purport to solve through institutionalising them in policy discourses and through funding their partial 'repair' (Bacchi, 2009; McLeod et al, 2016; Horton and Pyer, 2017). We maintain a critical approach to practices of youth governance that are framed in relation to youth in trouble, or youth as trouble, but at the same time we acknowledge that young people in contemporary society face new material and existential problems. Unprecedented inflation, the cost of living and the cost of education impact not just everyday life but curtail the possibility of future pathways including education and particular forms of employment. In addition to these impacts, climate change and what is now being called the sixth extinction (Eldridge, 2001) bring the very real possibility of the end of the world and the spectre of human extinction. The value of human life is fundamentally challenged by such threats.

The rising cost of post-secondary education in Australia is creating significant barriers for many young people, impacting their ability to gain skills accreditation and pursue career pathways. The increasing tuition fees and associated costs (such as textbooks, accommodation and living expenses) put a strain on students and their families (Thrower, 2024). Many young people are discouraged from pursuing higher education due to the financial burden, leading to fewer individuals gaining the qualifications necessary for skilled jobs (Salamanca, 2023). Reliance on student loans can lead to substantial debt, which may deter students from enrolling in post-secondary programmes, particularly those who cannot rely on significant family resources to offset the risks of this debt (McLaughlin, 2024; Thrower, 2024). Graduates may find themselves in a cycle of debt that affects their financial stability and career choices, as they may prioritise higher-paying jobs to pay off loans rather than pursuing fields they are passionate about. Rising costs of living disproportionately affect low-income and marginalised groups, exacerbating existing inequalities. Young people from disadvantaged backgrounds may not have access to the same educational opportunities as their wealthier peers, limiting their chances of obtaining necessary skills and qualifications. As fewer young people enter post-secondary education, there can be a mismatch between the skills available in the workforce and the demands of employers (Department of Education, 2024). This can lead to a skills shortage in critical areas, impacting the overall economy and hindering innovation and growth. The high cost of traditional post-secondary education may push some young people towards alternative pathways, such as vocational training or apprenticeships.

While these can be valuable, they may not provide the same level of recognition or career advancement opportunities as a university degree, limiting long-term career progression. The stress associated with financial pressures and the uncertainty of future employment can lead to mental health challenges among students. This not only affects their academic performance but also their overall well-being, further complicating their career pathways.

The increasing cost of post-secondary education in Australia has created a complex web of barriers that affect young people's ability to gain necessary skills and pursue meaningful careers, thereby impacting their future prospects and the overall workforce landscape. Working from within this context, this chapter examines the 'problem' of discourses of youth in trouble as detailed in the sociology of youth and education and then moves on to outline the contemporary social, financial, educational and environmental issues that are real problems in the lives of young people today. We argue that young people need to be understood as agentic, and that arts practices need to be seen as a direct expression of their agency.

Creative education and ethical surveillance

> Perfect actors, being natural artists, they [school students] will assume for the moment – and for the moment only – anything we insistently demand, be it respect, silence, obedience, adult etiquette or even affection. (Mearns, 1940/41: 14)

Although the topos of 'problem youth' in youth studies is largely a post-war phenomenon, reflecting the rise of a consumer economy in Western countries with its new cultural infrastructure for young people with disposable incomes, in the field of educational theory young people's *ethics* have been a problem since the earliest development of public education in the mid 19th century. One of the great achievements of post-Foucauldian scholarship has been to demonstrate that creative education emerged as a distinctively modern response to the problem of ethical development (Hunter, 1988; Bennett, 1998; Brook, 2015).

A key problem for the 19th-century designers of the public school system concerned the moral development of a new class of children – overwhelmingly working class and from diverse religious backgrounds – who through various acts of Parliament would be removed from the labour force and required to attend school. 'Moral development', a key goal of reformers, was problematic not because such children had low morality but because in deferring to the authority of the teacher, children tended to dissimulate their true nature, thus making it impossible for teachers to gauge the moral work to be done. In a mid-1800s treatise on school design, *The Training System, the Moral Training School, and the Normal Seminary*, school planner David Stow proposed that dedicated playgrounds – a novel technology in school design – would support the teacher in their task of ethical invigilation:

> The true character and dispositions are best developed at play with companions similar in years and pursuits … A play-ground is in fact the principal scene of the real life of the children … the arena on which their true character and dispositions are exhibited … Amidst this busy scene, the trainer must be present, not to check, but to encourage youthful gaiety. All is free as air, and subject only to a *moral* observation of any particular delinquency, the review of which is reserved for the school gallery. (Stow, 1850, quoted in Hunter, 1988: 35; original emphasis)

According to Ian Hunter, creative and cultural education in Anglophone education systems brought the ethical technology of the playground into the classroom. Cultural and creative activities – such as the reading and writing of poetry or performance of plays – were pedagogic techniques for encouraging the student to reveal their true self through their 'personal' and 'expressive' responses, as well as engaging them in a guided process of active self-reflection and correction (Meredyth, 1991; Smith, 1991; Patterson, 1993). Such pedagogic technologies (Foucault would call them 'apparatuses') included specialised facilities (playgrounds, art rooms, writing classes), routines (playground monitors), social settings (peer-based discussion, performances) and pedagogic techniques (the teacher's *encouragement* of *expressed personal experience* outside of any knowledge framework: 'There are no right answers here!'). The annexation of creative education to the development of *personal skills* was foundational to the creation of compulsory public education systems in the UK and Australia, skills that would come to be regarded as essential to 20th-century citizenship in liberal capitalist societies.

A striking example of Hunter's argument is found in the emergence of creative writing as a school subject in the US during the 1920s and '30s. This was the heyday of the progressive education movement, when popular educational philosophers such as John Dewey would promote the value of freedom and creativity for the school curriculum. Dewey proposed that '[t]he child is already intensely active, and the question of education is the question of *taking hold of his activities*, of giving them direction'; such activities are 'natural resources, the uninvested capital, upon which the growth of the child depends' (Dewey, 1956 [1899]: 36, 48; our emphasis). Dewey also offered suggestions on how writing studies might be refigured in the light of such a theory: 'Reading and writing, as well as the oral use of language, may be taught in a *related* way, as an outgrowth of the child's social desire to recount his experiences and get in return the experiences of others' (Dewey, 1956 [1899]: 56; original emphasis). That is, learning is a social activity with psychological motives that can be harnessed by the teacher; for Dewey, educational practice needed to be 'psychologised'. Two years before Dewey's bestselling *The School and Society* (1899), the educational psychologist Edward L. Thorndike published the results of his experiments on animal learning as *Animal Intelligence.* In this work, Thorndike reported the findings of his experiments in incentive-based and non-imitative learning in monkeys, finding that learning might be facilitated by the indirect training offered by specially designed enclosures. A key quotation from this work gives an indication of the more 'disciplinary' forms of pedagogy that were capable of being articulated with the goals of progressive education:

> Now every observant teacher realizes how often the cleverest explanation and the best models for imitation fail. Yet often, in such cases, a pupil, if somehow enticed to do the right thing, even without comprehension of what it means … will finally get hold of it … The best way with children may often be, in the pompous words of an animal trainer, 'to arrange everything in connection with the trick so that the animal will be compelled by the laws of his own nature to perform it'. (Thorndike [1898], quoted in Cremin, 1964: 112)

Often cited as a founding work of behavioural psychology, *Animal Intelligence* was squarely addressed to the emerging field of education studies and influenced a whole generation of educators who increasingly turned to creative approaches (Cremin, 1964: 113).

The work of Thorndike and Dewey was fundamental to the educational theory of Hughes Mearns, an educational researcher who developed creative writing classes at the experimental high school at Columbia University in 1917–19. In his massively influential report on his new creative classes, 'Creative youth: how a school environment set free the creative spirit' (1925), Hughes Mearns suggests that 'nothing in all the teacher's art can equal in potency the effect of the pupil's own contemporaries' (Mearns, 1925: 91) and even boasts that 'of formal group instruction there was none': 'The poem is passed around and fought over, but the teacher is only one of many voices, each striving to be heard. In that hurried give-and-take, *bombast, posing, unclear or insincere thinking, are laid bare* in language more instructive than any adult could contrive' (Mearns, 1925: 18; our emphasis).

Into the space vacated by instruction will come not only the uninhibited creative productions of 'even the shyest of aspiring youth' but also the necessary group ethos that will itself, if well supervised, perform the necessary work of pedagogy (66). In Mearns's descriptions of the contagious nature of creative inspiration, his point of view in fact shifts to that of his students:

> Consider that the writing of poetry has never been with us a classroom exercise but really a by-product … Conferences, such as were had, were snatched between 'periods' or in breathless perambulations in halls and on stairs. Our poetry, we always felt, was something we did for its own sake, and that naturally we should use our own time for it. (Mearns, 1925: 18)

Here we can see how the creative writing educator is to engage students in peer-based personal development. Extra-curricular spaces are both the outcome *and the support* of this commitment, deepening the pedagogy through personal investment that continues after the student has left school.

'Young people' in research

Young people are, in the first instance, a figure of discourse that is highly variable across institutional contexts. Marketing professionals seek to uncover new markets, while advertising creatives seek to make them. Government health departments research young people to improve services, while global tech companies undertake research and development (R&D) to develop new platforms for social media, educational courses and video games. Fashion designers study young people to draw inspiration for new collections, political parties study young people's concerns to develop election strategies and sociologists and psychologists develop 'reach-out' programmes and age-appropriate therapies.

Young people are variously constructed as a new type of consumer, as digital natives, as creative innovators, as prone to risky behaviour, as concerned about the future of the environment, as resilient, as vulnerable and so on.

Research on young people condenses fears and hopes, desires and ideologies, in a manner that often seeks to understand and prepare for the future. It is for this reason that research on digital technologies is often focused on the uses made of them by young people. Young people are, in a very important sense, an experimental population for developing new approaches. As technology plays a major role in articulating social and historical breaks, it is not surprising that it is often associated with a break in generations. The disruptions to the social landscape that make it hard for young people to reproduce the lives of previous generations – a characteristic of modernity that subtends the historical emergence of the concept of generations – can be partly addressed by looking to the new possibilities that come with such breaks.

To be young is to be identified, whether by oneself or others, in a particular way. It is for this reason that sociologists note a difference between biological and social age, with the latter being a matter of context-based judgements. For Pierre Bourdieu, 'youth' is always constructed in relation to the 'not young' as a site of struggle around social resources, such as social recognition, work status and financial security. The (self-)perception of youth, as of generations generally, is itself a symbolic positioning vis-à-vis others which has 'as its issue the transmission of power and privilege between generations'. Bourdieu cites that key theme of modernity – the search for the 'new' – as a key driver of this struggle:

> There are times when the search for the 'new' – through which the 'new come' (who are also, most often, the youngest biologically) push the 'already arrived' to the past, to the overtaken, to social death ('it is finished') – intensifies, and where, at the same time, the struggles between the generations reach a greater intensity: these are the moments when the trajectories of the youngest and the oldest collide, where the 'young' aspire 'too early' to the succession. (Bourdieu, 1993 [1978])

Youth arts and media as governmental intervention in post-industrialising economies

While creative practice has served a disciplinary function in educational settings since the development of public education systems in the 19th century (Hunter, 1988), the idea that it might address issues in youth employability specifically is very recent. The policy shift from employment to 'employability' since the 1970s, during which Western governments abandoned policies of full employment in favour of an expansion in access to post-compulsory education, was accompanied by a decline in broad-based manufacturing and the appearance of 'youth unemployment' as a new type of problem. It was during this period that the modern form of youth arts emerged, a subset of community arts that stressed the role of creative art and media in social integration, including the inculcation of employability skills (Hawkins, 1991; Brook, 2012).

Within this formation, access to creating culture was always tied, as Gay Hawkins notes (1991), to governmental agendas for the reform of problem populations. An indicative text of the era is the satirical skit 'Nozin' around' that parodied the discourse of youth media and its disciplinary role in channelling young people into work. The skit, performed by Ben Elton and Christine Ellerbeck, was a meta-TV segment in the first episode of a popular early 1980s British TV series *The Young Ones* (S1, E1, BBC, 1982–84). 'Nozin' around' is presented as a TV pilot for a new youth media program and is watched in the episode by the university student and anarchist Rick in the loungeroom of his London house share. On screen, the show's host Baz (played by Ben Elton) describes the program's intent:

> Me and my mates thought that TV just wasn't 'now', right … so we thought we'd have a program just for us, right, and this is it … a program *for* YOUNG ADULTS, made *by* YOUNG ADULTS. And concentrating on all the subjects that YOUNG ADULTS are interested in … like … UNEMPLOYMENT.

'Nozin' around' takes place in a TV studio youth disco with MCs Baz and Maggie dancing while they describe youth unemployment in circular bureaucratic terms ('Basically, the problem is this … if you can't find a job then you're out of work, and that means only one thing … unemployment'). The MC escorts the camera through the disco to meet an elderly careers officer, 'Roland Percival' (played by Anthony Sharp). 'If you're on the dole, go and see Rol', says Baz, to which Roland replies 'I should mention you do have to have a degree.'

The program abruptly ends when Rick kicks in his TV.

The critical purpose of 'Nozin' around' was to present youth media as a *ruse* which obfuscates the structural issues in national labour markets that have produced 'the problem', such as the Thatcher government's attacks on industry that produced widespread unemployment in the 1980s. That this satire of youth media took place *within* a TV show marketed at young people was a reflexive gesture towards the ambivalent position of youth media and the new opportunities within the UK's burgeoning cultural industries of the 1980s. *The Young Ones* is not at all concerned with unemployment but rather the creative lives of young people engaging with education (a student share house). *The Young Ones* showcased the talent of a new generation of creatives, notably Ben Elton, Rik Mayall,

Adrian Edmondson, Dawn French and Jennifer Saunders, all of whom became household names in British comedy in the 1990s. Indeed, in the 1980s the UK's creative sector itself was being touted as a field of employment and business opportunity (Flew, 2012), one that progressive government agencies, such as the Greater London Council, actively supported. *The Young Ones* celebrated the recuperation of time outside labour through subcultural style – the show is full of punks, headbangers, hippies, goths, rude boys – even as it acknowledged the commercialisation of such spaces, as in Alexei Sayle's song about Doctor Martens boots in S1, E2 ('Pretty soon everyone will be moving / to the sound of one beat / Thanks to Doctor Martens / They'll be Dancing in the Streets').

In the harsher social security landscape of the 21st century, the show's ability to distance youth unemployment as potentially a bureaucratic problem is perhaps its most dated aspect. The celebration of youth subculture as a temporary existential solution to the real-world problems confronted by young people seems unviable today. As Sayle's song about Doctor Martens suggests, such solutions already seem nostalgic. The signifiers of solidarity were always-already commodities; social youth identities were already markets in development. Such a critical reflexivity in the field of youth arts, we suggest, is foundational. Partly this is to do with the critical sensibilities of youth arts workers, but it is also because the field is administered to a very great extent by young people themselves, who must navigate the complexities of representing a cohort to which they belong and whom they are offered professional opportunities to manage. This can be ambivalent, as professional creative industry and social development agendas are not necessarily aligned, as when young people seeking industry careers are offered youth arts work. Arts manager Marcus Westbury describes his ambivalent relationship to the professional opportunities of youth arts work in mid-1990s Australia, a period when youth arts was expanding:

> It began when I was twenty-one with an act of faith. A group of friends and co-conspirators each put $500 towards renting a warehouse and establishing an under-resourced, over-ambitious and unfunded arts and media collective, Octapod. This was in Newcastle in the mid-1990s, and youth unemployment was running at about 40 per cent. (Westbury, 2006: 11)

Westbury's work in fringe arts in Newcastle in the mid 1990s – a post-industrial city just north of Sydney – when he was in his early 20s led to his engagement as an internet manager by a national youth arts media project. This project was the LOUD festival initiated by the late-Keating government, funded by the Commonwealth Department of Communications and the Arts and managed by the Audience Development and Advocacy Division of the Australia Council. Through television, radio, print and online media, the LOUD festival brought the media-based creative works of young (12–25 years) artists and media makers to a national audience of an estimated 1 million Australians and leveraged significant financial and in-kind support from media sponsors. By engaging the Australia Council as manager, this was a festival that sought to override the separation of the arts from mass broadcast media and *model* a programme for professional arts and media training through brokering links between content producers and the cultural industries. Westbury himself would co-present on ABC TV's *Recovery* program, and as the only festival staff member in the target age range (that is, young), he would be engaged as the 'public face' of the festival in the media (Westbury, 2006: 12).

The LOUD festival sought to harness the growing arts sector interest in 'youth arts' in the 1990s (Hunter, 1999) for Keating-era cultural industries arts policy agendas. However, as a top-down, government initiative, the LOUD festival was perceived to lack credibility and as being patronising towards its target demographic: '*Youth* is not what you want to be, and is the last context in which you wish to see your work presented' (Westbury, 2006: 13). In his reflection on his role in the festival as a 'professional token youth', Westbury writes: 'The role is to represent the presence of the group of people that you nominally represent. Within reason, your role is to actually represent them, but more often than not your role is to cover the idea that they are represented. How you do it is up to you' (2006: 13).

This chapter has traced how young people have been framed across different discourses, as problems to be managed, as risks to be contained, as subjects in need of ethical formation and as experimental populations for future-oriented governance. From 19th-century school reforms that sought to monitor morality, through 20th-century investments in creative education and progressive pedagogy, to late 20th-century youth arts initiatives linked to employability and the cultural industries, youth have continually been imagined and governed through overlapping assemblages of discipline, opportunity and hope. At the same time, we have seen how these frames remake the very issues they claim to address, institutionalising the 'problem of youth' in ways that reproduce inequality while offering only partial solutions.

Yet, as we have argued, the social, material and existential challenges that young people face today – rising costs of education, precarious employment, widening inequalities, climate collapse and the spectre of extinction – are not simply discursive productions. They are real and urgent conditions shaping the lives and futures of young people. To reduce youth to figures of risk or objects of intervention is to miss the complexity of how they navigate these conditions and to overlook their capacity for agency.

Reframing youth agency requires holding together this double perspective: a critical awareness of the ways youth have been problematised and governed, and an affirmation of the ways young people act, create and reimagine their worlds in response to the crises that surround them. Arts practices are central here, not only because they have historically been entangled with projects of moral regulation and employability but because they also open spaces for self-expression, collective identification and new forms of political and ethical action. When we attend to creative practice as a direct expression of youth agency, we begin to see young people not only as subjects of governance or objects of concern but as actors in their own right, shaping futures in ways that unsettle established categories and offer possibilities beyond the 'problem youth' frame.

In this sense, the challenge for youth studies is not simply to critique how youth are governed but to engage seriously with the practices through which young people exercise agency in a world marked by profound precarity. By reframing youth agency through creativity, expression and collective action, we can begin to tell a different story about what it means to be young today: one that recognises young people as agents of cultural, social and political possibility in times of extraordinary uncertainty.

THREE

The futures of skills, work and credentialing

The history of the problem of young people, skills and the future of work

The 'problem' of young people's transitions from school to work, and how governments, businesses, schools, communities and individuals can manage young people's education, training and employment pathways, has been a significant feature of youth policy since the early 1980s. This is especially evident in Australia and in many of the over-developed, high-income economies of the Organisation for Economic Co-operation and Development (OECD) and the European Union. As we discuss in this chapter, at various times this 'problem' has taken on greater importance, including during and after the GFC of 2008–9 and in the still unfolding context and consequences of the COVID-19 pandemic and the social and economic lockdowns of 2020–22.

One of the challenges at these times of crisis is to keep in mind the longer-term trends and trajectories that characterise this 'problem' and to reflect on the dominant ways issues are imagined, and why. For example, Australian federal and state policy responses to changes in youth employment and labour markets since the 1970s have been diverse. They have played out in the Victorian regional city of Geelong, a former 'manufacturing powerhouse' that had, like many other 'rust-belt' towns and cities in Australia (Newcastle in New South Wales and Elizabeth in South Australia), the US (Detroit), the UK (Newcastle) and elsewhere, been 'smashed' by the flight of capital and jobs as a consequence of processes of neoliberal globalisation since the 1980s (Noonan and Kelly, 2019). Beyond the particularities of place in deindustrialising contexts such as Geelong, our interests are in exploring the concepts of 'employability skills', 'innovation' and 'enterprise' (21st-century skills) and asking how these contested, often ambiguous, concepts emerged, at different times since the 1980s, as promising to provide a 'solution' to the problem of youth unemployment in the context of these processes of neoliberal globalisation. In brief, a number of points can be made about how the problem of young people and the future of work has been imagined during this period.

First, transformations to the economy, youth labour markets and young people's education, training and employment pathways since the 1980s have been fundamentally structural. Despite this, most policy responses, and the politics of these transformations, have focused on individual young people's 'employability skills', 'innovation' and 'enterprise' (21st-century skills), how to develop these and what happens to those young people who don't have these 'skills'. Second, there is not one single 'youth labour' market. Rather, in different rural and regional areas, towns and cities and economic sectors ('legacy', 'emerging' 'platform based', 'creative and arts based'), there are different education, training and employment opportunities for young people. These different labour market opportunities and forms of economic activity require different skill sets. Different young people, both individually and as members of 'populations' such as First Nations, migrant and refugee, culturally and linguistically diverse, neuro-diverse, 'working-class' young men and women, face different challenges and opportunities on their education, training and employment pathways and in developing the 'skills' that different labour markets demand.

Beyond what we have called the 'event horizon' of the COVID-19 pandemic (Carbajo and Kelly, 2023), there is significant evidence in many of the high-income economies of the OECD and the EU, and in many of the medium- and low-income economies, which suggests that there has been an amplification of the challenges and inequalities born by young people (European Youth Forum [EYF], 2020a and b; Fergusson and Yeates, 2021). Even though COVID-19 has not affected the physical health of young people to the extent it has with older populations, the unfolding social, economic, political and policy crises that the pandemic triggered have altered most dimensions of their lives, provoking new debates about the 'problem of generations'. These impacts can be identified in relation to young people's education, training and employment pathways, their mental health and well-being and in restrictions to previously taken-for-granted 'rights', including movement, assembly and sociality (EYF, 2020a and b; OECD, 2020). For example, in a paper where they report on their interviews with young hospitality workers in Australia who were impacted by COVID-related, public health lockdowns in mid 2020, Cook et al (2021) highlight how prior to the pandemic many of these young people's experiences of these labour markets were overwhelmingly characterised by uncertainty and precarity. They suggest that the uncertainty the pandemic produced makes it very difficult to predict longer-term impacts. In this space of uncertainty, the pandemic, they argue, should be imagined not only as a 'health crisis that impacts on precarious workers' but as 'a crisis of precarious work itself'. A crisis largely hidden from community understandings prior to the pandemic, but one which has been 'experienced and negotiated in terms of the relationship between inequality and uncertainty that has emerged in the context of labour market precarity among youth' (Cook et al, 2021: 15).

We develop these points in what follows. These ideas, which have featured heavily in sociologies of young people and education during this period, have both informed our development of the Vital Arts research project and how we see the research being able to contribute new knowledge to this ongoing problem. In Chapter Two, we argued that while young people have been variously framed as problems to be managed, the challenges facing young people, far from being discursive productions, are very real and urgent. Our account of how globalised labour markets have become increasingly individualised, precarious and risky expands this argument. The meanings associated with work, the values and economies that it signals, have changed in ways that increasingly demonstrate the character and extent of the choices an individual can imagine and/or make. For some, 'vocation is a privilege' (Bauman, 2005). For others, work/labour remains 'toil and drudgery' (Trinca and Fox, 2004). This 'history of the present and future' of work has been profoundly impacted by the pandemic. We identify 'global grammars of enterprise', which increasingly demand young people develop entrepreneurial, aspirational dispositions towards their present and future participation in labour markets. In making this argument, we introduce the concept of 21st-century skills. The concept, and its identification of a range of foundational literacies, competencies and character qualities, plays a central role in the work of the Vital Arts project. This idea of 21st-century skills and how they can be identified, developed and measured has come to feature prominently in dominant policy discourses about young people, education, training and employment pathways. In our concluding section, we build on these themes to critically reflect on what has been called the 'fetishistation' of skills and the apparent narrowing of the focus on debates about young people and their education, training and employment pathways to a catalogue of discrete foundational literacies, competencies and character qualities.

Beyond the 'work society'?

Mateus arrived in London at 13 with a guitar case that had more stickers than strings. São Paulo still clung to his vowels, and his mother's WhatsApp voice notes filled the small kitchen of their flat in Tottenham with instructions about everything from rice to resilience. School was a blur at first: new slang, new weather, new rules, but music translated easily.

That was where he met Oliver.

Oliver had been born in London, in a part of the city where houses leaned politely away from the street and gardens were curated rather than grown. His parents spoke about universities the way others spoke about holidays: as destinations assumed, not imagined. He played drums competently, confidently and had been told since childhood that he was 'well rounded'.

They formed a band almost accidentally. A borrowed rehearsal room, a bassist who came and went, and long afternoons learning covers before attempting their own songs. They called themselves 'Static Weather', a name Mateus liked because it felt like contradiction: noise and stillness at once.

They were good friends.

In sixth form, the future began to arrive, not as a possibility but as a demand.

Oliver's world tightened into applications. Personal statements were drafted, redrafted, then sent off to UCAS like sealed declarations of intent. His teachers spoke to him in a language of trajectories: 'Russell Group', 'internships', 'networks'. His parents discussed 'options', though all options seemed to orbit stability.

Mateus watched this process as if through glass.

He had forms too, but they were different. Residency paperwork. Proof of address. Letters that required translation, not just of language, but of legitimacy. His mother worked two jobs; stability, for them, was measured week to week. University was possible, but it came wrapped in questions: fees, visas, the right to remain.

Still, they played.

Music was the one place where the future loosened its grip. In rehearsal rooms that smelled of dust and electricity, they were not yet divided by outcomes. Oliver's drumming was precise, structured; Mateus's guitar drifted, improvised, searching. Their songs began to take shape around this tension.

By the final year, the divergence was unmistakable.

Oliver secured an offer from a university his parents approved of. There was relief in it, not joy exactly, but confirmation. The path extended forward in a recognisable line: degree, internship, graduate scheme. The labour market, for him, still resembled what sociologists once called a work society: a system where effort mapped onto reward, where institutions buffered uncertainty, where identity could be anchored in occupation.

Mateus's path was less linear.

He applied to university too, but each step carried risk. Would his status allow him to stay? Would he be able to afford it? He took part-time work: first in a café, then delivering food across the city at night, the guitar case replaced by a thermal backpack. His phone became both boss and supervisor, assigning shifts, tracking performance, calculating worth in real time. What Beck would call a risk society was not an abstraction for Mateus. It was the texture of daily life.

The responsibility to manage uncertainty fell almost entirely on him. There was no guarantee, no institutional cushion that felt secure. Instead, there was an expectation, both spoken and unspoken, that he would become entrepreneurial: flexible, adaptable, self-investing. He learned to optimise his hours, to brand himself for small gigs, to maintain an online presence that might translate into opportunity.

Work was no longer a stable anchor. It was a shifting terrain.

They noticed the difference most clearly one evening after rehearsal.

Oliver had just returned from a university open day. He spoke about facilities, societies, the 'experience'. There was a sense, almost invisible, that the system would hold him, that it was designed to absorb him into its rhythms.

Mateus nodded, then checked his phone. A shift had just opened up. If he accepted it within 30 seconds, he'd earn a little more that week.

'You coming?' Oliver asked, gesturing to the pub.

Mateus hesitated. The shift would cover next month's travel card.

'I can't', he said. 'Work.'

Oliver frowned – not dismissively, but uncomprehendingly. 'Can't you just ... not take it?'

Mateus smiled, but it didn't reach his eyes. 'Not really.'

Their band continued, but it changed.

Rehearsals became harder to schedule. Oliver's time was structured around deadlines and plans; Mateus's around availability and demand. The same concept: work operated differently in their lives.

For Oliver, work was still tied to identity in a traditional sense. It promised meaning, status, a narrative of progression. It was, as Beck argued, central to moral being – something through which a life could be evaluated.

For Mateus, work was fragmented, precarious. It did not promise salvation; it demanded management. Each decision carried risk, and each risk was his to absorb. There was no stable 'outside' to work, no clear opposition – only the constant negotiation of survival within it.

One night, after a small gig in Camden, they packed up in near silence.

'You're good, you know', Oliver said finally. 'Like, properly good. You could make something of this.'

Mateus laughed softly. 'Yeah. Maybe.'

But the words hung differently for each of them.

For Oliver, 'making something' implied a pathway: a series of steps that could be followed, however competitive. For Mateus, it implied exposure: to failure, to instability, to a system that offered no guarantees.

They stood outside, the city humming around them.

'Do you ever think', Mateus said, 'about not working? Like ... just doing something else?'

Oliver frowned, instinctively. 'What do you mean?'

'I don't know. Just ... not everything being about jobs. About proving something.'

Oliver shook his head slightly. 'That's not really how it works, is it?'

Mateus looked out at the traffic, the endless motion of it.

'Yeah', he said. 'I guess not.'

By the time summer ended, Oliver left for university. His departure was marked by a small gathering, polite congratulations, a sense of transition that felt almost ceremonial.

Mateus stayed.

He enrolled in a local course, continued working, continued playing when he could. His life did not pivot; it accumulated.

Risks layered on risks, decisions folding into one another without resolution.

They kept in touch, but less frequently.

Years later, if you asked them about that time, they would tell similar stories, about music, about friendship, about London. But beneath those stories, something else persisted.

A divergence.

One shaped by a system that once promised stability through work, and another shaped by a world in which that promise had fractured: replaced by uncertainty, by individualised responsibility, by the demand to constantly manage risk.

And somewhere in that divergence, the old idea of work: as salvation, as identity, as measure, began to loosen its hold.

Not entirely broken.

But no longer unquestioned.

And as I have mentioned the word labour, I cannot help saying that a great deal of nonsense is being written and talked nowadays about the dignity of manual labour. There is nothing necessarily dignified about manual labour at all, and most of it is absolutely degrading. It is mentally and morally injurious to man to do anything in which he does not find pleasure, and many forms of labour are quite pleasureless activities, and should be regarded as such. To sweep a slushy crossing for eight hours on a day when the east wind is blowing is a disgusting occupation. To sweep it with mental, moral, or physical dignity seems to me to be impossible. To sweep it with joy would be appalling. Man is made for something better than disturbing dirt. (Oscar Wilde, *The Soul of Man Under Socialism*, 1891, cited in Thomas, 1999: 413)

Oscar Wilde's disdain for manual labour is aligned with the fetishisation of 'soft' and transferable skills we see in contemporary labour markets. A key feature of the ways paid work and youth labour markets have been transformed over the last 40 years is in the emphasis on abstract labour, branding and the marketisation of selfhood as part of joining the labour force. Further, for many young people employment is increasingly part time, casual, 'precarious' and 'gig based' and 'platform enabled'.

This precariousness should be understood as a structured phenomenon. The ideal, the promise and the skill of being flexible, of flexibility, is different from living a life that is precarious. It is different because the nature and consequences of choices are different for different populations in different locations with different labour market opportunity structures (Bauman, 2001, 2005).

Zygmunt Bauman (2004) offers powerful analysis of processes of globalisation and modernisation in which hundreds of millions of people around the globe are rendered 'supernumerary', 'of no use', 'surplus to requirements' and condemned to live what he terms 'wasted lives'. Unemployed, marginalised young people face the real prospect of the social and material oblivion that awaits those whom the competitive, rationalised, globalised labour markets of 21st-century, flexible capitalism consider redundant (Kelly and Harrison, 2009). Developing a passionate, entrepreneurial form of selfhood in formerly marginalised, unemployed young people has, as its endpoint, its destination, both employment and a sense of meaning and purpose in young people's lives. But while this is important, what room do these ends leave for other possibilities for what a life might mean? Do these ends also suggest that any work is 'good' work? That there might, for example, be little sense in making distinctions between work as toil and drudgery and work that promises meaning, purpose and 'self-fulfilment'? Are labour markets, and their tenuous, precarious offer of salvation from material and social oblivion, the only spaces in which meaning and purpose can be found? If so, is this meaning and purpose also tenuous and precarious?

In seeking to explore these and other questions, we turn to a number of ideas/concepts from Ulrich Beck's *Brave New World of Work* (Beck, 2000). In that book, structured as it is by his 'Brazilianisation' thesis, Beck argued that the labour markets of the overdeveloped West were being transformed through the movement from the work society to the risk society (Furlong and Kelly, 2005). In the work society, the promise of salvation, meaning and purpose was to be realised in relatively stable labour markets that were rendered governable alongside forms of social insurance, welfare and regulation. A risk society, however, is characterised by forms, and understandings, of uncertainty, precariousness and risk that locate responsibilities for identifying and managing risk with individuals largely via the development of entrepreneurial forms of selfhood. As Beck (2000: 10) argued:

> The extent to which work is part of the modern European's moral being and self-image is evident from the fact that, in Western culture, it has long been the only relevant source and the only valid measure for the evaluation of human beings and their activities … Work has become so omnipotent that there is really no other concept opposed to it. Hence, any attempt to break out of this value-circle of work lays itself open to the accusation of cynicism … Any vision worthy of the name must therefore cast off this spell of work, and begin by breaking the taboo on any antithesis to the work society.

The ways in which Bauman has written of 21st-century work as an aestheticised object of consumption and choice can also give insight into these dimensions of the processes of self formation in and through the ability to find and secure employment in increasingly precarious and individualised labour markets.

In a discussion of what he argues is a shift from a society of producers to a culture of consumers, Bauman (2007: 28) defines *consumerism* (as distinct from *consumption*) as a form of 'social arrangement that results from recycling mundane, permanent and so to speak "regime-neutral" human wants, desires and longing into the *principal propelling and operating force* of society'. These forces facilitate and structure processes of social reproduction, stratification, integration and 'the formation of individuals'. In making up persons, *consumerism* gives shape to identities, processes of identification and differentiation and provides direction and purpose to the making and enacting of 'individual life policies'. In this formulation, 'consumerism is an attribute of society', not of individuals. The development of consumerism requires that individual desires, fantasies and longing must be 'detached (alienated) from individuals' – thus mirroring a particular way of imagining the roles played by labour capacity in energising a producer/industrial society. Once alienated from the individual, desire, fantasy and longing need to be 'recycled/reified', as Bauman (2007: 28) argues, into forces external to the individual which then propel 'the "society of consumers" in motion and keeps it on course as a specific form of human togetherness': an individualised, even privatised, form of human experience with the capacity for 'setting specific parameters for effective individual life strategies and otherwise manipulating the probabilities of individual choices and conduct'. An individualised, consuming life is a life that, paradoxically, given the values accorded to individualised choice and freedom, takes its form and its purposes from structuring processes that compel the person to be free, to make choices, to carry the responsibilities for the consequences (burdens, benefits) of making choices.

Throughout history, jobs have existed that bring with them different levels and kinds of satisfaction and fulfilment. Meaning, purpose and a sense of achievement are to be found more readily in some jobs than in others. For Bauman

(2005: 32–3), this reality charts what he sees as the movement from a work ethic to an aesthetic of consumption. Within the terms of a Calvinist/Puritan work ethic, no forms of work were considered to be 'deprived of value and demeaning'. All forms of work had the potential to add something to 'human dignity and all work equally served the cause of moral propriety and spiritual redemption'. In this sense, all kinds of work were on an equal footing. The work ethic functioned, in some respect, to enable all to see in their toil, their labour, the potential for a satisfaction to be found in their calling. However, as Bauman argues, when work becomes an aestheticised object of consumption, the belief that all work has an equal value is diminished, even removed: the 'status occupied by work, or more precisely by the job performed, could not but be profoundly affected by the present ascendancy of aesthetic criteria'. It is in this sense that we can imagine that work has 'ceased to be the focus of particularly intense ethical attention in terms of being a chosen road to moral improvement, repentance and redemption'. In a culture of consumption, the ways in which we imagine and experience work come 'first and foremost under aesthetic scrutiny. Its value is judged by its capacity to generate pleasurable experience.' When work is devoid of a capacity to generate an aestheticised, pleasurable experience, when it fails to deliver some form of 'intrinsic satisfaction', then such work is increasingly imagined and experienced as if it was 'devoid of value'. An *aesthetic scrutiny* and *evaluation of work* emphasises differences and distinctions between forms of work and particular jobs and 'elevates certain professions to the rank of engrossing, refined objects of aesthetic, indeed artistic experience, while denying to other kinds of renumerated livelihood-serving occupations any value at all'. At the same time, other means for understanding and valuing work 'cannot withstand the competition and are not powerful enough to save work from condemnation as useless or even demeaning for the aesthetically guided collector of sensations'.

In this sense, when work that is, by all accounts, toil and drudgery (Ehrenreich, 2002) is undertaken by persons who are held to be responsible for conducting themselves as an enterprise, then we can imagine such a self as a failing enterprise: 'No fully fledged consumer would conceivably agree' to do these sorts of jobs on 'her or his own will, unless cast in a situation of no choice (that is, unless his or her own identity as a consumer, a free chooser, has already been forfeited, withdrawn or otherwise denied)' (Bauman, 2005: 34).

In a consumer culture, values such as freedom, choice, mobility, flexibility and vocation become powerful structuring forces that give shape to the sense of the self as an enterprise. Work which is 'rich in gratifying experience, work as self-fulfilment, work as the meaning of life, work as the core or the axis of everything that counts', work as *better than sex* (Trinca and Fox, 2004), work as the 'source of pride, self-esteem' is the marker of vocation as privilege (Bauman, 2005: 34). Vocation as privilege has become a 'distinctive mark of the elite, a way of life the rest may watch in awe, admire and contemplate at a distance'. In these spaces, the trick, as Bauman (2005: 34) suggests, is not to 'limit work time to the minimum' but to 'efface altogether the line dividing vocation from avocation, job from hobby, work from recreation; to lift work itself to the rank of supreme and most satisfying entertainment'.

Under the regime of the work ethic, the moral value attributed to the calling, to the duty attached to doing any job well, meant that an individual's, even a population's orientation to this duty was a powerful signal of character, of virtue, of worth. *She's got a great work ethic! He just lacks a work ethic!* In many respects, this moral overtone is still explicit in the ways in which distinctions continue to be drawn between the deserving and undeserving poor, those apparently willing to work and those who are not. Seeing work as an aestheticised act of choice, a matter of consumption, of the capacity to freely choose that which will give meaning, purpose and satisfaction, does not replace this moral imperative. Rather, it displaces this moral judgement onto the acts of choice and the self, as enterprise, who exhibits a seemingly limited capacity to exercise choice. These moral judgements, argues Bauman (2005: 36), enable us

> to believe that the voluntary 'flexibility' of the work condition freely and enthusiastically chosen by those at the top, and once chosen cherished and keenly protected, must be an unqualified blessing to everybody else, including those to whom 'flexibility' means not so much freedom of choice, autonomy and the right to self-assert, as lack of security, forced uprooting and an uncertain future.

It is these properties of individualised choice and freedom, and the significant incentives and imperatives to imagine one's life choices, chances and options in terms of these values, that are so powerful in giving shape to the sense that the self is, ought to be, an enterprise; and an enterprise that finds in differing work-related capacities, desires and fantasies a means to materialise the character and contours of this ongoing, never-ending project. Here, *What do you do*? becomes less an opening gambit in conversation that might locate a self and more an indication of the current state of the self as enterprise – a state that might be failing, might appear as successful, but a state that is, as we are all aware, parlous, precarious and always in need of close, intense, reflexive scrutiny and care.[1]

Work in the sociologies of youth has made a significant contribution to examining the affective, embodied, gendered, aesthetic and classed dimensions of new forms of labour of/for young people. David Farrugia and colleagues (2018), for example, explore how young people mobilise embodied affect to negotiate employment, particularly in customer-facing hospitality roles in labour market sectors that are characterised by part-time, casualised, precarious 'gig work' (see also Noonan and Kelly, 2019). They suggest that the modes of bodily comportment mobilised in these service industries are 'marked by ethnicity, gender and class in ways that designate particular young people as "appropriate or inappropriate employees"' – the 'white, slim, young, unwrinkled, typically heterosexualised body' is the ideal figure in these interactive industries (Farrugia et al, 2018: 274). With its mobilisation of conventional heterosexual norms of attractiveness, the labour of young women also often involves sexualised aspects of performance (Farrugia et al, 2018: 274–5).

In addition, those young people 'who are able to demonstrate middle-class manners and cultural tastes are favoured employees of high value' in various of these customer-focused service industries (Farrugia et al, 2018: 275). Two key elements of the analysis presented by Farrugia et al are of interest here. First, they suggest that in the shift from manufacturing to service-based economies the products of labour become largely 'immaterial': 'This labour is a critical aspect of what has been called the "new economy"... in which the shift from manufacturing to service economies makes the production of signs, symbols, sensations and interactions into central economic activities' (Farrugia et al, 2018: 275). Second, drawing on the work of Michael Hardt and Antonio Negri (2004) and Gilles Deleuze and Felix Guattari (2007), they suggest that the production of immaterial goods is made possible because labour, here, has become 'affective'. In this sense, 'affects include experiences of fun, pleasure, conviviality or "atmosphere"', and the experiences and atmospheres that are produced through the embodied practices of workers in the course of their interactions with customers can contribute to the creation of value and profit for employers (Farrugia et al, 2018: 275). Farrugia et al's work is suggestive of new approaches to and understandings of the experiences of young people in precarious, globalised labour markets – particularly those labour market segments that display and require the performance of a certain form of attractive, desirable 'youthfulness':

> In particular, the study of affective labour suggests new ways of understanding how youth itself is shaped by labour in a context of employment insecurity, how young embodied subjectivities reflect the social organisation and practice of work in the contemporary economy, and how youthfulness itself operates as an input into the production of value in contemporary capitalism. (Farrugia et al, 2018: 285)

In a number of recent collaborations (Carbajo and Kelly, 2019, 2023; Goring et al, 2023), we have built on these sociologies to develop an analysis of how the future of work is imagined in various 'official' discourses, the behaviours and dispositions and types of personhood that young people should develop in relation to these official accounts of imagined futures and the central role played by what we have called 'global grammars of enterprise' in structuring these imaginaries. In the following section, we will draw on aspects of these collaborations to situate an account of the emphasis that is currently placed on the concept of 21st-century skills in these grammars of enterprise.

Young people, the future of work and global grammars of enterprise

In recent years, a growing literature in sociologies of work, education and youth has sought to explore aspects of how neoliberal capitalism, precarious work and education and training policies and systems create demands for young people to be and become more 'enterprising' (Howie and Campbell, 2016; Serrano and Martin, 2017; Holdsworth, 2018; Oinonen, 2018; Ikonen and Nikunen, 2019; Walsh and Black, 2020).[2] David Farrugia (2019: 1088), for example, has identified two 'manifestations of the post-Fordist work ethic', which he characterises as 'subjects of achievement' and 'subjects of passion'. Farrugia suggests that these 'ideal types' could be used to describe young people's 'classed aspirations for self-realisation through work'. In his research with young people in a number of unemployment 'hotspots' in Australia, Farrugia (2020) reports on the ways in which many young people articulate the prospect of decent, rewarding work through explicit and significant distinctions, in terms of a sense of self, between a 'job' and their aspirations for a 'career'. In the context of the precarisation of work in post-Fordist contexts, Farrugia (2020: 1–2) argues that sociological research on young people and work should engage with 'the concept of "career" not merely as a biographical structure, but as a grammar of the self that provides a vocabulary through which contemporary youth articulate projects of self-realisation in line with the requirements of the labour force'.

As Farrugia (2020: 14) argues, 'career has become a vocabulary for talking about the cultivation of the self' and a means of 'responding to the neoliberal imperative to work on the self as a way of navigating the labour market'. Indeed, for many young people 'career' has become a key referent for the 'deliberate cultivation of employability, self-improvement, personal development, uniqueness, aspiration and passionate commitment'.

Long before the COVID-19 crisis emerged – at a time in which labour markets were becoming increasingly globalised, and precarisation processes were altering young people's working and living conditions – global, national and regional networks of public and private agencies were deploying particular understandings of enterprise and entrepreneurship as the primary mechanisms to deal with young people's marginalisation, exclusion and un/under-employment. In these settings, 'enterprise' and 'entrepreneurship' have been proposed as individualised, but institutionally driven, strategies to improve young people's employability (Serrano and Martín, 2017). More importantly, 'enterprise' has been fostered as a 'code of conduct' by which young people can develop and perform a form of personhood that promises to make them more employable in increasingly precarious labour markets

(Kelly, 2006, 2013). The neoliberal logics and rationalities at play here suggest that everything works better – more efficiently, more creatively, more productively – if it is run as an 'enterprise'. Translated to persons, this kind of imperative claims that to achieve a certain type of labour market and employment 'success', individuals need to imagine themselves as 'enterprises' and develop behaviours and dispositions shaped by a market-driven rationality and ethos (Foucault, 2008; Lazzarato, 2012; Lorey, 2015; Bröckling, 2016).

Since the 1990s, various players, including business schools, management consultants and globalising organisations, have played significant roles in what Nigel Thrift (2005) has termed the 'cultural circuits' of capitalism. These cultural circuits have been able to process, package and place management knowledge in all kinds of fields by providing mobile formulas and models that can be applied in, and transferred to, many diverse situations. The Global Entrepreneurship Monitor (GEM), for example, prepares a global census of entrepreneurship and produces and circulates a range of indicators of entrepreneurship. Based in a global network of universities and research institutes, GEM provides regional analyses, international comparisons and rankings of entrepreneurship. These and other practices have collaborated in joining particular understandings of 'entrepreneurship', the 'future of work' and 'young people' to create a powerful artefact of expertise (Kelly, 2000).

Our contribution to these theoretical discussions proposed the metaphor of grammars of enterprise (Carbajo and Kelly, 2019, 2023) to better understand the norms and regulations of this doctrine of enterprise and how it is expanded and reproduced by its circulation in global and local networks. The concept enables us to identify, examine and analyse a number of things, including the shifting, always-strategic power relations between governmental discourses of 'enterprise' and the performances and actions of enterprise – the enterprising behaviour and dispositions of persons and groups, the 'vernacular', local, particular 'translations' of the ideas of entrepreneurship – that organisations and young people perform in particular places (Carbajo and Kelly, 2019, 2023). The use of grammar here does not have its foundations in Derrida's (1976) concept of grammatology. Rather, it is closer to a looser use of grammar by authors such as Braudel (1987), Virno (2001/4) or Martuccelli (2007) and is a way of addressing the use of institutionalised and formalised representations of entrepreneurship (Foucault, 1980).

The measures implemented by agencies and institutions of government in different parts of the world that aim to foster various entrepreneurial projects are crucial elements of global grammars of enterprise. These elements operate as an 'apparatus' (Foucault, 1980) that puts into circulation, or re-signifies, concepts in a way that, far from being neutral, are, in part, inherently 'moral' (Sayer, 2000; Kelly and Pike, 2017). These different agencies give shape to a political, juridical and administrative field of plausibility or reality, where some possibilities are promoted while others become unthinkable. At this time, it is useful to briefly revisit elements of this argument, and the contexts from which it emerges, through a sketch of the ways in which, for example, the European Commission (EC) and the Foundation for Young Australians (FYA) imagine – in different though often similar ways – how it is that entrepreneurship, entrepreneurialism and 'enterprise skills' promise to provide young people with the capabilities, attributes and dispositions necessary to thrive in 'new work orders' (FYA, 2015).

During the last 20 years, and more so in the aftermath of the GFC of 2008–9 and the so-called Great Recession in much of the European Union, the EC has implemented a range of incentive mechanisms to promote entrepreneurship among individuals, businesses and society as drivers of European economic recovery and long-term growth. For example, the 'Entrepreneurship 2020 action plan: reigniting the entrepreneurial spirit in Europe' (EC, 2012) has three main objectives: (1) developing entrepreneurial education and training; (2) creating the right business environment; and (3) identifying and promoting role models and reaching out to specific groups, including young people. These objectives create a sense that 'enterprise', as an institutional product or artefact, is also a personal quality (characterised by such things as risk taking, initiative, creativity), and/or that individuals can be imagined and 'made up' to embody and perform the qualities of an enterprise (Armstrong, 2005: 6).

It is in these contexts that 'youth' has emerged as a paradigmatic case of governmental processes – a 'biopolitical program' (Foucault, 2008) – that seek to produce and promote entrepreneurship. In the 'Entrepreneurship 2020 action plan', the EC (2012: 6) suggests that

> [w]hether or not they go on to found businesses or social enterprises, young people who benefit from entrepreneurial learning, develop business knowledge and essential skills and attitudes including creativity, initiative, tenacity, teamwork, understanding of risk and a sense of responsibility. This is the entrepreneurial mind-set that helps entrepreneurs transform ideas into action and also significantly increases employability.

The FYA is an influential Australian third-sector, youth-advocacy organisation. Since 2015, FYA has commissioned research on the changing world of work and the disruptions to work that it identifies as stemming from the social, economic, technological and policy drivers of, and responses to, 'automation', 'globalisation' and 'collaboration'. These reports, which comprise FYA's New Work Orders series, focus on the education and training regimes that can meet the 'needs' of this changing world of work and on the attributes and characteristics of the forms of personhood that young people must develop to meet these changes.

FYA's research and advocacy response to these disruptions has been framed by a sense that governments, education systems, businesses and community agencies need to develop approaches to young people's education and training that foster and enable young people to develop what it sees as 'enterprise skills'. For FYA (2017: 5), enterprise skills are 'transferable skills that enable young people to engage with a complex world and navigate the challenges they will inherit'. These skills 'are not just for entrepreneurs; they are skills that are required in many jobs. They have been found to be a powerful predictor of long term job success.' What are often called generic, soft or 21st-century skills include: 'Problem solving; Communication skills; Digital literacy; Presentation skills; Critical thinking; Creativity; Financial literacy.' 'We need', suggests FYA (2017: 5), 'the next generation of young Australians to be more enterprising, innovative and entrepreneurial to drive our nation's future.' The aspiration here is for young people to be able to embody the enterprise and entrepreneurialism that many organisations and governments have come to see as structuring the purposes of education at the start of the 21st century. We will develop a number of these points in the following section in a more detailed examination of the concept of 21st-century skills.

21st-century skills

As our discussion in the previous section indicated, there is an increasing focus in policy, education and community discussions on the apparent skills and capabilities that young people will need to develop and demonstrate in order to 'thrive' in the complex, changing, precarious and uncertain labour markets of the 21st century. There is also much debate about these skills and capabilities: What are they? How do we understand these so-called 21st-century skills/capabilities? Where/when/how can they be developed in different parts of compulsory and post-compulsory education (primary, secondary, further/technical/higher education)? In turn, there is significant debate about how these capabilities, once identified, then developed, can be measured. And much debate about whether, for example, accredited vocational education training programmes have the capacity to develop and assess for them in a competency-based training framework (see, for example, Australian Council for Educational Research [ACER], 2013; Jones, 2018; Lamb et al, 2018).

In a 2018 report that canvases a number of challenges for Australian vocational education and training systems, Anne Jones (2018), from the Centre for the Study of Higher Education at the University of Melbourne, outlines both the context of profound changes in labour markets, especially for young people, and the sorts of capabilities young workers need to develop in order to be employable in these labour markets: 'We do not know how work and employment opportunities will change in the near future. Predictions range from "forecasts that nearly half of jobs in advanced economies may be automated out of existence" to confidence that high-level vocational skills will be more important than ever in the digital world' (Jones, 2018: 2). In this context, Jones (2018: 2) claims that 'people will need educational breadth as well as occupational depth to adapt and thrive as industries and society change'. In this account, Jones (2018), drawing on policy development by the European Union, identifies the need for young people to acquire and develop the kinds of '21st-century capabilities' that are

> necessary to remain globally competitive and to best prepare individuals for lifelong employment. These comprise high-level technical skills, core skills and a range of capabilities referred to in the EU as transverse capabilities – 'the ability to think critically, take initiative, problem solve and work collaboratively will prepare individuals for today's varied and unpredictable career paths … particularly entrepreneurial skills'. (Jones, 2018: 4)

Stephen Lamb et al (2018: 2), from the Centre for International Research on Education Systems at Victoria University in

Figure 3.1: 21st-century skills

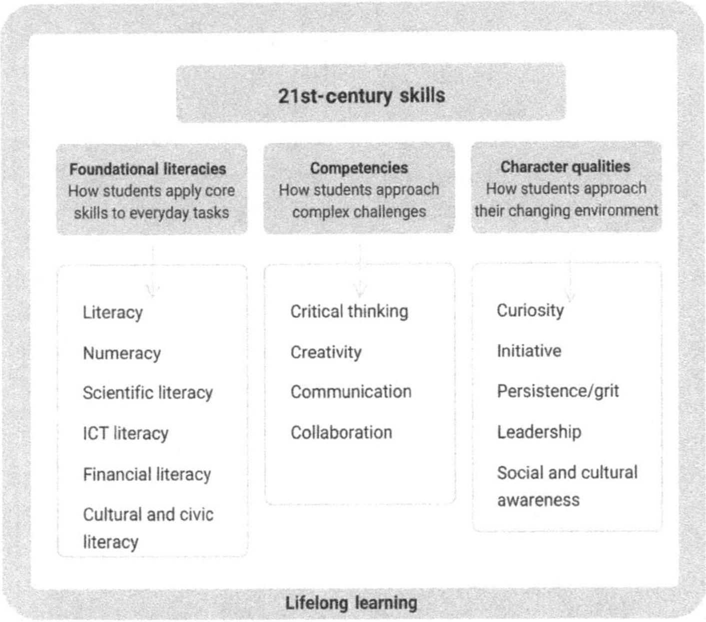

Source: Adapted from WEF (2016: 4)

Melbourne, report on some of the work they have done in defining, categorising and assessing these sorts of capabilities. As they indicate: 'While there may be general agreement in the literature that 21st-century skills are important, there is far less agreement as to what these skills are; whether they are malleable; whether they have any effect on other outcomes; and how they might be measured' (Lamb et al, 2018: 2).

The WEF (2016, see Figure 3.1) is just one of many organisations that continues to try to identify and classify the ranges of behaviours, competencies, skills, dispositions and capabilities that apparently comprise 21st-century skills.

In these spaces of debate and uncertainty about 21st-century skills, we have found the WEF's model to be a useful though not unproblematic way to frame a variety of discussions. It is useful at this stage for its relatively clear representation of the 'skills' that an individual young person should have, develop, be able to use. One challenge, however, is that many of these 'skills' – the so-called 'competencies' and 'character qualities' in particular – might also be thought of as 'personality traits' or 'intrinsic' parts of a person's 'make-up'. And, therefore, not that easy to teach, or for young people to 'acquire' and develop, and/or to capture or measure.[3]

Recognising this dilemma, Lamb et al (2018: 4; see Table 3.1), present a 'taxonomy' of different clusters of 'competencies' (Cognitive, Intra-personal, Inter-personal) comprising a list of commonly used terms that name 21st-century skills in each of these clusters and a list of corresponding cognitive and personal abilities.

This sort of classification captures a sense of the range of 'capabilities' that are most frequently described when people are talking about 21st-century skills. At the same time, when we encounter models and taxonomies such as those developed by the WEF and Lamb et al, our concerns relate to how these models and taxonomies do very little work in moving beyond an abstract, decontextualised naming of such things as, for example, 'critical thinking', 'problem solving' and/or 'leadership'. There is, as many have argued, a 'social life' to the acquisition, development and use of these skills and capabilities that is missing from these models. Jill Blackmore (1992: 355–6), for example, has suggested that policy discourses on such things as young people's employability skills discount, even ignore the 'social life' of these skills – 'how the skills are acquired (training/experience), who possesses the skills (male/female, adult/youth) and in what context these skills are used (public/private)' (see also Goring, 2023).

We can see how the commonly identified 21st-century skill of 'creativity' is a central element of the vocabularies of this grammar. As we have suggested (Carbajo and Kelly, 2023), the concept of 'creativity' figures prominently in contemporary

Table 3.1: 21st-century skills clusters, with associated cognitive abilities and personality traits

	Cluster	Terms used for 21st-century skills	Main cognitive ability/ personality factor
Cognitive competencies	Cognitive processes and strategies	Critical thinking, problem solving, analysis, reasoning/argumentation, interpretation, decision making, adaptive learning, executive function	Main cognitive ability factor: fluid intelligence
	Knowledge	Information literacy (research using evidence and recognising bias in sources), information and communication technology literacy, oral and written communication, active listening	Main cognitive ability factor: crystalised intelligence
	Creativity	Creativity, innovation	Main cognitive ability factor: general retrieval ability
Intra-personal competencies	Intellectual openness	Flexibility, adaptability, artistic and cultural appreciation, personal and social responsibility (including cultural awareness and competence), appreciation for diversity, adaptability, continuous learning, intellectual interest and curiosity	Main personality factor: openness

Table 3.1: 21st-century skills clusters, with associated cognitive abilities and personality traits (continued)

	Cluster	Terms used for 21st-century skills	Main cognitive ability/ personality factor
	Work ethic/ conscientiousness	Initiative, self-direction, responsibility, perseverance, productivity, grit, Type 1 self-regulation (meta-cognitive skills, including forethought, performance and self-reflection), professionalism/ethics, integrity, citizenship, career orientation	Main personality factor: conscientiousness
	Positive core self evaluation	Type 2 self-regulation (self-monitoring, self-evaluation, self-reinforcement), physical and psychological health	Main personality factor: emotional stability (opposite end of continuum from neuroticism)
Inter-personal competencies	Teamwork and collaboration	Communication, collaboration, teamwork, cooperation, interpersonal skills, empathy/perspective taking, trust, service orientation, conflict resolution, negotiation	Main personality factor: agreeableness
	Leadership	Leadership, responsibility, assertive communication, self-presentation, social influence with others	Main personality factor: extraversion

Source: Lamb et al (2018: 4)

youth education, training and work policy spaces. For example, in Australia the 'Melbourne declaration on educational goals for young Australians' (Ministerial Council on Education, Employment, Training and Youth Affairs [MCEETYA], 2008) was a significant framing document that evolved out of previous declarations (the Hobart [1989] and Adelaide [1999] declarations) by Australia's MCEETYA. The Melbourne declaration has since shaped the policy agenda for education and training and youth affairs in Australian states, territories and at the federal level. Goal 2 of 2 of the declaration had the aim that all young Australians would 'become successful learners, confident and creative individuals, and active and informed citizens'.

Of interest at this time is the naming of 'creativity' and its positioning in relation to other ideas about 'confidence', 'activity' and 'informed citizenship' as being a preferred character attribute of the individual and a primary goal of education in the 21st century. The behaviours and dispositions that are characteristic of *confident and creative* young people include that they:

- have a sense of self-worth, self-awareness and personal identity that enables them to manage their emotional, mental, spiritual and physical wellbeing;
- have a sense of optimism about their lives and the future;
- are enterprising, show initiative and use their creative abilities;
- develop personal values and attributes such as honesty, resilience, empathy and respect for others;
- have the knowledge, skills, understanding and values to establish and maintain healthy, satisfying lives;
- have the confidence and capability to pursue university or post-secondary vocational qualifications leading to rewarding and productive employment;
- embrace opportunities, make rational and informed decisions about their own lives and accept responsibility for their own actions (MCEETYA, 2008: 9).

As George Morgan and Pariece Nelligan (2018: 15) have argued in *The Creativity Hoax: Precarious Work and the Gig Economy*, while workers' creativity was considered of little value in Fordist capitalism, the notion of creativity as a 'productive energy' has become one of the most important and elusive elements of new work orders. In this sense, creativity is reframed as the ability to imagine, identify or even produce a gap in the 'normal order of things' as a means to identify and extract value. Creativity becomes something that can be framed and measured and, as such, commodified and monetised. The contemporary demands for persons to be and become 'creative' intersects with the need to act in an entrepreneurial way, pointing towards a 'renewed' economisation and marketisation of the possibilities of human and non-human actors/materials generating unforeseen combinations and relations (Redmalm and Skoglund, 2020). We will expand on this argument in Chapter Five, demonstrating that while 'creativity' has been lauded as an essential skill for producing value in an innovation-based economy, it has long been viewed as a complex skill to develop in educational contexts. In doing so, we will further contextualise the social life of this skill in the specific context of youth arts and education.

Conclusion: Beyond the skills fetish?

> The rise of a strictly economic interpretation of lifelong learning which demands from individuals that they keep upgrading their skills and qualifications in order to remain employable, is an example of the workings of a 'politics of learning' in which structural issues concerning the global labour market are entirely addressed in terms of individuals and their learning. (Biesta, 2011: 3)

In this chapter, we have explored the extent to which labour markets have become increasingly precarious for young people. In the face of these changes, there have been growing demands on young people to develop entrepreneurial dispositions towards their participation in these labour markets, what we have termed the 'global grammars of enterprise'. Although workforce participation has always featured in 'the problems of youth', at the start of the 21st century it has taken on a new urgency. For instance, in OECD economies, the decline of manufacturing from the 1970s, the hollowing out of middle-skilled jobs through the rise of the 'hour-glass' skills economy and evidence of declining returns to human capital due to labour market crowding have only intensified. These structural features have been met with new discourses on the knowledge society, creative skills and the digital economy (Fehér et al, 2017). These developments have radically altered both the social and policy landscape that confronts young people today, affecting their aspirations and understanding of what is possible. Through the Vital Arts project, however, we offer an innovative, anti-marketisation reading of micro-credentials and the possibilities and pathways created by our community distribution strategies for the micro-credentials. In Part II of this book, we will explore these readings further.

PART II

The creative industries: partnerships, practices, diverse economies

FOUR

Promising partnerships and technology futures

Introduction

Tom liked to say the Venice Biennale ran on precision. In reality, it ran on improvisation disguised as planning. He had spent 15 years inside its machinery: negotiating artists, managing installations, smoothing over the quiet frictions between curators, funders and publics. But this year was different. The programme leaned heavily towards interactive and participatory works: pieces that depended on audience movement, responsiveness, co-creation. Less object, more encounter. And encounters were messy. 'Who's running Pavilion 7?' he asked, scanning a spreadsheet that looked more like a risk register than a staffing plan.

'Still vacant', his assistant replied. 'We've interviewed three candidates. Strong degrees. Weak ... everything else.' Tom knew what that meant. They could write about participation; they couldn't manage it. They understood theory, not contingencies. When a sensor failed, or a participant misused the work, or a queue became a crowd: things fell apart. He had started to suspect that the pipeline itself was the problem.

A month earlier, under pressure and mild desperation, Tom had signed the Biennale onto a micro-credential network run by an industry connected start up. It was pitched as a way to access 'practice-ready talent': workers who accumulated verified digital badges in specific competencies rather than relying solely on degrees. Tom had been sceptical.

Badges sounded like gamification. Like shortcuts. Like something HR would love and operations would regret. Still, the system was live now. A dashboard populated with profiles: skill clusters, endorsements, evidence portfolios. Not essays about art, but videos of installations, logs of troubleshooting, multilingual annotations. He clicked through them late one evening, more out of obligation than hope. That's when he found Tran ... Tran's profile didn't follow the usual arc. No completed secondary education. No university degree. Instead: a dense constellation of micro-credentials. 'Interactive systems setup'. 'Audience flow management'. 'Live troubleshooting for media installations'. 'Multilingual facilitation (Vietnamese/English/Mandarin)'. Each badge linked to evidence, short clips of exhibitions, testimonials from small galleries, documentation of pop-up shows assembled under tight constraints.

It wasn't polished.

It was convincing.

Tran had learned art work sideways.

They had arrived in Europe with family, moved between cities, picked up work where it was available: artist-run spaces, community festivals, temporary exhibitions that required more doing than discussing. Someone had shown them how to wire a projection system; someone else how to reset it when it failed. Languages came through necessity: Vietnamese at home, English in school, Mandarin through co-workers and audiences.

The digital badges came later.

A friend had mentioned the creds programme that recognised specific skills. Tran didn't need abstraction; they needed recognition that travelled. Each badge was a way of making their experience legible to institutions that otherwise filtered them out. They worked through modules at night, uploading evidence from jobs that rarely left a paper trail. It wasn't education as Tom understood it. It was accumulation.

The interview was brief. Tom expected to lead. He didn't.

'Tell me about a time something failed during an installation', he began.

Tran didn't hesitate. 'Which kind of failure?' Tom blinked. 'Any.'

'Hardware, software, or people?' Tran asked. That was the moment he understood the difference. They spoke for 40 minutes. Not about theory, but about sequences: what breaks first, what breaks next, how to prioritise under pressure. Tran described a participatory work where audience members triggered sound through movement. The sensors lagged; the crowd grew impatient; the artist panicked.

'What did you do?' Tom asked.

'I turned it off', Tran said simply. 'Then I explained the concept without the tech. Slowed the room down. Restarted in stages.'

Tom nodded slowly. That wasn't in any manual.

By the time the Biennale opened, Pavilion 7 was no longer a problem.

It was, unexpectedly, a success.

The work itself was complex: a multi-user interactive installation requiring coordination between digital interfaces and physical participation. Early testing suggested it would fail under real conditions.

It didn't.

Tran moved through the space with a kind of quiet authority. They spoke to artists in the language they preferred: switching between English, Vietnamese and Mandarin without pause. They translated not just words, but intentions. When audiences hesitated, they guided them. When systems faltered, they fixed them, sometimes invisibly, sometimes by reconfiguring the experience altogether.

Tom watched from a distance.

This was what he had been missing. Not knowledge *about* participation, but the capacity to sustain it in real time.

Midway through the festival, a visiting curator approached Tom.

'Who's managing that pavilion?' she asked. 'It's one of the few that actually works.'

Tom gestured towards Tran.

'She's ...' he paused, then corrected himself. 'They're from our new recruitment stream.'

'Which university?' the curator asked reflexively. Tom smiled slightly. 'Not the usual route.' Later, reviewing reports, Tom noticed something else. Incidents in Pavilion 7 were lower than average. Audience satisfaction was higher. Downtime was minimal. But more interestingly, the qualitative feedback shifted. Visitors described feeling 'guided', 'understood', 'included'. The work was doing what it was supposed to do, not just functioning, but connecting. Tran's role was not supplementary. It was structural. On the final night, as installations began their slow dismantling, Tom found Tran packing cables into labelled cases.

'You did good work', he said.

Tran shrugged lightly. 'It's what I do.'

Tom hesitated, then asked the question that had been forming all month.

'Why didn't you finish school?' Tran looked up, not defensive, just matter of fact. 'I needed to work.' Tom nodded. In another system, that might have been disqualifying. In this one, it had simply redirected the pathway. The micro-credential network had not replaced degrees. It had complicated them.

For Tom, it reframed what counted as expertise. The badges were not abstractions; they were compressed signals of practice, backed by evidence. They allowed someone like Tran, who operated fluently across technical, social and linguistic domains, to be visible within an institutional system that typically excluded them.

For Tran, the badges did something else. They redistributed risk. Instead of relying on a single, high-stakes credential (a degree they could not access), they built a portfolio of smaller, verifiable competencies. Each badge was a unit of recognition, a way to enter spaces that would otherwise remain closed.

As the Biennale closed, Tom updated his hiring strategy.

Degrees would remain.

But they would no longer dominate.

Because somewhere between the spreadsheets and the installations, between the plans and the contingencies, he had learned something precise: in a field defined by interaction, unpredictability and live publics, the ability to DO: to adapt, translate and troubleshoot in real time was not secondary to knowledge. It was the condition of possibility for everything else. And in that shift, the distance between institutional expectation and lived capability had, briefly, narrowed.
A win, not just for Tom. But for the system he was slowly learning to reconfigure.

This chapter focuses on how digital micro-credentials catalyse organisational partnerships within the youth arts sector. In understanding how partnerships figure in micro-credential development, this chapter considers micro-credentials as a 'promissory discourse', a concept we borrow from the sociology of technology. Promissory discourses make 'assurances that something (e.g. an event, experience, change) *will* occur in the future' (Petersen, 2018: 192). In the case of emerging technologies, promissory discourses draw together a range of stakeholders and help to create and legitimise audiences and markets for new technologies. In this way, they have been described as 'performative' in that the very act of creating assurances in the present helps to bring forth a future yet to come (Petersen, 2018; Holcombe-James et al, 2022).

A promissory discourse draws together a number of organisational actors, such as arts managers, young creatives and researchers, as well as funding resources and digital learning designers, to produce a discourse about the future, one which calls forth commitments to a shared but uncertain process of value creation. The process of framing that discourse, deciding which actors to enrol and what platform architectures to create, the crafting of research pitches, of critiques no less than meeting transcripts and PowerPoints, produces a promissory discourse that calls forth commitments. Such commitments are mutable, contingent and negotiated.

From such an approach, digital micro-credentials are not reducible to either educational critiques of 'neoliberal instrumentalism' for the platform economy (Wheelahan and Moodie, 2022) or corporate consultancy visions of enlightened social progress through digital disruption. Rather, they must be understood in the first instance as the catalyst for organisational and sector change.

In this chapter, we briefly review the key claims of the sociology of technology, applying them to digital micro-credentials as a form of promissory technology that catalyses partnerships around expectations and future outcomes. We then provide an overview of arts partnerships and policy in Australia, including the role of the federal arts agency Creative Australia (formerly known as Australia Council for the Arts) as a key agent in arts research. We then return to our case study of youth arts micro-credential development to see how various youth arts organisations and young people themselves describe the value of micro-credentials.

The problem space of digital badges

In 2010, the software company Mozilla partnered with the MacArthur Foundation and the Carnegie Foundation for Advancement of Learning to hold the first 'Mozilla drumbeat festival' in Barcelona. This festival – held annually ever since – was a showcase for 'Learning, Freedom, and the Web' and promoted open-source digital badges as a way to democratise learning, especially for coders and web developers. In a subsequent discussion paper by the Mozilla Foundation and Peer 2 Peer University, called 'Open badges for lifelong learning', the authors asked readers to '[i]magine a world where your skills and competencies were *captured* more granularly across many different contexts, were *collected* and associated with your *online identity* and could be *displayed* to key stakeholders *to demonstrate* your capacities' (Mozilla Foundation and Peer 2 Peer University, 2012; our emphasis).

This was the foundation for open-source digital badges that, it was claimed, would empower independent communities to recognise informal learning online. Badges were eminently social and defined thus: 'A "digital badge" is an online record of achievements, tracking the recipient's communities of interaction that issued the badge and the work completed to get it' (Mozilla Foundation and Peer 2 Peer University, 2012).

Open digital badges were imagined as non-proprietary and network based, being based in the valuing practices of the communities that underpin peer recognition. But unlike the quality of peer recognition – an intangible social phenomenon some sociologists describe as symbolic capital – badges have a material form. They might be physical badges, such as patches or pins that testify to some skill level or membership.

The concept of an online digital record of achievements was anticipated by Microsoft in 2005 when it created its 'achievements' tokens for gamers on the Xbox 360 platform (Jakobsson, 2016). As Jakobsson notes, the precursor to this was the use of physical badges to signal achievement in game play. In the 1980s, and prior to the internet, several videogame companies issued physical patches to domestic videogame players if they posted the company a photograph of the leader board on their television screen that proved their high score (Jakobsson, 2016). Today, the term 'digital badge' refers to image files with embedded metadata that are linked to a host site (typically a platform provided by the issuer, or a third-party service, such as Badgr or Credly), where further information is available about the badge recipient (such as the activity they undertook) and the badge issuer.

'Open badges for lifelong learning' imagines four learner profiles as a way of describing the social needs and problems that open digital badges might address. It asks us to imagine Kareem, a 16 year old who loves films and robots but struggles in school because he doesn't understand how academic learning relates to real life:

> Luckily, he's been able to pursue his interests through more informal learning opportunities with his peers through his local Learning Network after-school program: he's made short films in a series of youth-oriented digital media workshops, mentored some younger kids at the local FabLab, and participated in a hands-on, sustainability-focused 'hackfest' competition. (Mozilla Foundation and Peer 2 Peer University, 2012: 1)

Then there is Sara, an 18-year-old web developer who has been coding since she was 13. She is under pressure to go to uni but doesn't see the point as the courses are well beneath her skill level:

> She has taken a few open education courses through Peer to Peer University on specific new technologies and learned a great deal both in the course work as well as the peer community she met there. And yet she has nothing formal to put on a resume, which has made it impossible to get in the door at any employer. (Mozilla Foundation and Peer 2 Peer University, 2012: 1)

There is also Jin,

> a 28-year old artist and writer … who completed part of an associate's degree at the local community college in management but dropped out to pursue her creative interests full-time. She is an active participant in a local art community through online social networking, city meet-ups and annual conferences and shows. (Mozilla Foundation and Peer 2 Peer University, 2012: 2)

And finally Antonio, a 39-year-old publishing professional who was recently laid off and wants to pivot to environmental policy. 'He feels he has learned a lot that is relevant to the new field throughout his undergraduate education, work experience and personal projects, but he has nothing to show for it.'

All four profiles relate to creatives (coders, artists, film makers, publishers) who are independent, informal learners who have skills that are not captured by formal qualifications and are consequently 'unrecognised' by labour markets. They are young, culturally diverse, skilled in professional creative fields (software, arts, media, publishing) and have some kind of problematic or interrupted relationship to formal education: it is too expensive (Antonio), redundant (Sara) or just unrelatable (Kareem and Jin). Such narratives not only identify an 'ideal type' of learning that open-badge communities might serve – adding to network-based peer-to-peer learning a form of portable online recognition of such learning – but also a 'problem space' that a new technology might address.

The paper proposes three key benefits of badges and the problems they overcome. They will (1) capture and translate learning across contexts, making skills acquired in one context visible within another (overcoming the problem of unrecognised skills); (2) motivate participation and learning outcomes, through acting as rewards to learners that incentivise them to undertake and/or complete an activity (overcoming the problem of the disincentivising effects of non-recognition); and (3) formalise and enhance 'existing social aspects of informal and interest-driven learning' through their contribution to community identity through peer recognition and belonging (overcoming the problem of low social capital – in both senses of community bonds and individual contacts – that results from unrecognised skills) (Mozilla Foundation and Peer 2 Peer University, 2012: 5–6).

Technology futures

In recent years, sociologists of science and technology have sought to understand how new technologies come about through shared understandings of the future. As with the founding Mozilla report on digital badges discussed in the previous section, new technology development involves discourses that both problematise the present and imagine the future. They seek to draw together actors around a discourse or problems and possibilities and strengthen this network through technologies that can give collaboration an enduring, material form. The study of 'expectations', 'future talk' and 'promissory discourses' in science studies is accompanied by concepts of 'the promissory economy' and the study of actors' 'projective capacity' as both a symbolic and material action (Borup et al, 2006; Mouritsen and Kreiner, 2016; Alper, 2019; Holcombe-James et al, 2022; Bazzani, 2023). Understanding such processes involves not only discourses and the material objects and relations they accompany but also the role of the future in *bringing people and things together* in an enduring form. As Borup et al write: 'Expectations are "constitutive" or "performative" in attracting the interest of necessary allies … and in defining roles and in building mutually binding obligations and agendas' (2006: 289). They ask researchers to enquire into how symbolic activity is 'materialised' in socio-technical arrangements: 'What are the routes of transmission between expectations, embodiment and materiality, and specifically the means by which promissory abstractions about the future take on substances, becoming materially embedded in structures, routines, systems, matters?' (2006: 292).

Promissory discourses are sites of socio-technical prolepsis, that is, *anticipatory* rhetorical gestures that seek to bring about the futures they describe through the process of technology development. In the case of our own research project, the technology of digital micro-credentials is combined with two further objects – 21st-century skills and youth arts programmes – in order to draw together social actors in a shared project that proposes to materially alter the future of young people.

Before a single badge is issued or a young person employed, the process of developing 'Digital micro-credentials' for the youth arts sector is a socio-technical assemblage that draws together people, organisations and digital systems to produce an outcome and a discourse about that outcome. Digital micro-credentials require partners to make promises to each other; and they also importantly make a claim to value, namely that participation in youth arts projects contributes to young people's skills.

Such projects cannot emerge *ex nihilo*. The Open Badges project of the Mozilla Foundation built on the success of the Peer 2 Peer Foundation, enthusiasm for Web2.0 as a distributed internet architecture for user-generated content and social network sites, as well as over a century of progressive educational theory in the US that, since the time of John Dewey, has always noted the value of project-based, creative and informal learning (for example, Cremin, 1964). Likewise, the Vital Arts project builds on assumptions about the value of industry partnerships in the Australian arts sector, as well as the shared understandings about the rationales for youth arts as a sector that can support young people's education and employment outcomes. Such institutional history is key to understanding how a field of sector agencies can converge around common understandings, including framings of the problem. In the following section, we describe the historical conditions for some of these assumptions.

Policy and partnerships

Arts agendas are routinely advanced through cross-industry as well as government partnerships, often across levels of government as well as portfolios, such as education, skills and training, regional development, city planning and so on. While such partnerships are generally sought after by arts sector agencies seeking to broaden stakeholder interest, they also come in for criticism for detracting attention from the interests of 'the arts'. The history of cultural policy is very much a history of debate about legitimate interests and hence the remit of cultural policy as such. There is no natural alignment between arts policy and agendas related to youth well-being, education or employment outcomes; and indeed, many arts lobbyists and researchers argue such agendas 'instrumentalise' the arts to the neglect of their intrinsic value for reasons to do with 'neoliberalism' (Morgan and Nelligan, 2018). Such accounts overlook the more fundamental nature of value, which is that there is no value in itself, only *value for* (Frow, 1995). The *process* by which specific value claims for (groups or interests) are articulated to understandings of the public good, and therefore general value, is intrinsically political. In the context of youth arts, diverse agents are drawn together to represent the interests of the sector, and by extension the interests of young people themselves. Such representations happen through policies and partnerships which, increasingly in the arts, collaborate with academic researchers to produce evidence-based studies to support sector initiatives.

Vital Arts and partnerships

Vital Arts was established as an ARC 'Linkage project'. The Linkage programme through the ARC has been designed to promote partnerships between academic researchers and industry and businesses and community organisations. According to the ARC itself: 'By supporting the development of partnerships, the ARC encourages the transfer of skills, knowledge and ideas as a basis for securing commercial and other benefits of research' (ARC, 2025). Partnerships are thus a critical component of this project, which has been designed from the outset to treat the youth arts sector as a co-producer of knowledge. However, the promise at the heart of these Linkage projects, of 'securing commercial and other benefits' through partnerships, is of course one in which ideas of value and benefit are inherently contentious.

Partnerships figure in this project through many forms. The research team is made up of researchers from multiple academic institutions, including RMIT University, Deakin University and the National University of Singapore, leading to collaborative cross-institutional partnerships. The research team also works closely with the arts industry in Australia, exemplified through the presence of Creative Australia, the federal arts council, as a major research partner on the project. There are four major youth arts and industry partners on the project: ATYP, The Push Youth Music Organisation, CMY and Future Foundations. In addition to financially contributing to the research project, these partner organisations are integral in supporting the research, design and implementation of the micro-credentials, and it is through these partner organisations that the micro-credentials are being tested and piloted. In the latter half of the project, the research team has also worked closely with the UK-based organisation 'CLOCK Your

Skills' on the design of the micro-credentials. The final major partnership in the project is the Action Research Industry Group, which is a consultative panel made up of experts from youth arts, education and industry.

Creative Australia (known as the Australia Council for the Arts until August 2023) is the federal government's arts investment and advisory body. The agency was given statutory authority in 1975 by Whitlam's Labor government in the tradition of the British model of arts funding, that is, one that addresses the failure of the market to support 'non-commercial' arts and culture with the provision of government subsidy through a competitive grants process (Hesmondhalgh et al, 2015: 108).

Research had long been a part of the organisation's ongoing activities, with key projects in Throsby's longitudinal Survey of Professional and Practising Artists and the National Arts Participation Survey.

This role was however catalysed by a significant period of defunding by the federal commonwealth government in 2015, when the Coalition government, under the then-Minister for the Arts and Attorney-General George Brandis, cut nearly $114 million from the Australia Council's budget and proposed that $110 million be diverted into a new National Programme for Excellence in the Arts. This National Programme would distribute funding at the minister's discretion and would, it was suggested, break the 'monopoly' of arts funding held by the Australia Council – wording that demonstrated the Coalition's discomfort with the relationship between the arts agency and its arts sector peers.

One of the effects of this funding announcement was job losses at the organisation, along with a profound destabilisation of confidence in its social and political position. No longer could the federal arts agency assume its role in the distributions of public investment in arts and culture, nor could it publicly celebrate its close relationship with artist peers in the sector. Under these changing conditions, the organisation began to diversify its portfolio relationships and to invest in research that would track the public value of arts investment beyond the arts sector. This period was also accompanied by significant private investment in arts sector research through the establishment of A New Approach.

The post-Brandis years of the Coalition government saw an expansion of research activities at the Australia Council to include those that demonstrated the impacts of public funding, along with the secondary, social benefits of arts investment as well, such as the benefits of arts programmes in schools, the health system and other cross-sectoral contexts.

The national cultural policy of the previous Labor government – a document called 'Creative nation' – had also formalised Creative Australia's research function, giving the agency a legislated mandate to conduct research on the sector and to evaluate the agency's programmes. These were important contextual shifts in the policy, social and political landscape, all of which contributed to a newly developing emphasis on research and evaluation. From this position, the size and reach of the council's research team grew, and in 2017 a new role was created that would broker and manage external research partnerships, most of which would be with academic researchers and many of which would be funded by the ARC: the 'Research Fellow and Manager of Research Partnerships' role.

This newly created role, which includes both academic and policy language in itself, would further strengthen the council's position in its generation of knowledge about the benefits of arts investment and arts engagement, along with its development of partnerships which were themselves a valuable resource. This position was a way to leverage the expertise that existed within the university sector while also securing cross-portfolio investment in the arts from education and training (through the ARC Linkage scheme).

The role exemplified an expansion of Creative Australia's focus in terms of research capacity while also securing its position through relationships beyond the sector and with other parts of the public sector. These were all shifts that were formalised and reinforced when the Labor government returned to power once more in 2022 and announced its new cultural policy early in the next year: 'Revive'. This document elevated the importance of research, of measuring the impacts of arts investment through a promised evaluation of the policy and with actions committed to research projects or consultations to support arts researchers in their work.

The document was also explicitly cross-portfolio in its positioning and ambitions, seeking to embed the arts, and an appreciation of the importance of arts and culture, within a network of intergovernmental and social relationships. Partnerships between the public and private sector were also an important new development, with the merger of Creative Partnerships Australia with the organisation, and a new focus on industry in the establishment of Music Australia and Writers Australia and the addition of private or commercial arts to the organisation's remit. This was a consolidation in many ways of trends that had been emerging over the previous two decades that had sought to link the arts sector to other sectors (with the lens of 'creative industries', 'the creative economy' and the idea of artists' 'transferable skills') and to use research to understand and explain the value of arts investment.

Alongside these developments at the federal arts agency, academia was increasingly expected to work with industry, with ARC Linkages as a mechanism for that work. Thus, Creative Australia and the university sector met in the middle, with a new regard for industry and for research to guide decision making and design of initiatives. The Vital Arts project exemplifies this changing position of research at Creative Australia. The Research Fellow and Manager of Research Partnerships role is a Chief Investigator on the Vital Arts project – and an important lynchpin in the project's relationship with the arts sector.

Promissory partnerships in practice

The promise of micro-credentials is often one of agility, low cost, speed and flexibility in both design and learning. The promise inherent within this discourse is of easy, uninterrupted value creation for young participants, employers and the youth arts sector. However, active engagement with industry partners through this project has demonstrated how these discourses can, in fact, be interrupted and challenged, creating both occasions for sector transformation and challenges to normative understandings of value. Rather than offering a high-speed pathway to skills accreditation, the collaboration between academia and industry has required a slowing down and drawing out of the micro-cred development process. The value of the micro-creds in the future is being brought forth through the collaborations and negotiations of industry partners throughout the research project. This is not a linear process: instead, partners who come from diverse parts of the sector are creating a shared understanding of value that requires constant renegotiation.

In thinking about the micro-credentials themselves as a 'promissory discourse', we explore the various ways that different actors have been mustered together to create a shared understanding of the value and potential of the micro-credentials. Partners on the project saw varied opportunities in their involvement. Several of the research partners from arts organisations saw the value in framing the micro-credentials around 21st-century skills, for example, because they felt this framework would give the arts sector and its workers a new language to talk about the programmes they are delivering. This would not only support outward-facing communication but also internal processes, such as evaluation and feedback.

Fraser Corfield from ATYP talked about how it can often be difficult to give young participants critical feedback during workshops and programmes. He saw that through the micro-credentials and the language of 21st-century skills, youth arts facilitators would have a new way of offering feedback to their students. For example, a facilitator could talk about what it takes to be *collaborative* or to engage *critical thinking* in relation to the craft or programme on offer and talk to young participants about whether they had demonstrated these skills. Corfield felt this would make the feedback process easier and less confrontational for facilitators by creating a shared language and framework for facilitators and participants.

Beyond participant feedback, Zoe Scrogings from Corrugated Iron Youth Arts discussed how the micro-credentials would help them to embed reflection more at an organisational level. She talked about how often youth arts organisations such as Corrugated Iron are too busy running programmes to have enough time to engage in adequate reflection and evaluation processes. This has obvious negative effects, where the value of the programmes cannot be precisely articulated for participants and funding bodies, despite that value appearing self-evident to those within the sector. For Corrugated Iron, the micro-credentials offered a unique opportunity to negotiate and talk about the impact their programmes were having on young participants using a new and transferable language of 21st-century skills. This would mean that the micro-credentials do not just have value in giving the young people a language to talk about their skills but create a new set of relations between young people, youth arts organisations, the youth arts sector and funding bodies, where understandings of value are more easily negotiated and articulated through a shared language.

For Christine Evely of the Australian Centre for the Moving Image (ACMI), these interventions were not exclusive to the youth arts sector but had the potential to redefine education more broadly. Christine talked about the micro-credentials giving teachers a new way of doing things and stressed that this potential should not be lost in the design of the micro-creds:

> I just think that micro-creds have that potential, probably even more than ChatGPT actually, that there's a lot of

> potential here to change pedagogy at the secondary level, and the tertiary level too perhaps, but particularly secondary and to get teachers thinking about different ways of doing things. So, I'd hate that to be lost in the whole thing. (Christine Evely, ACMI)

Many of the partner organisations wanted to frame their programmes through this lens of broader social good. Effective evaluation was tied to being able to prove how their programmes were contributing to social cohesion, youth employability and broader policy agendas, and this appeared as a driving factor for their involvement in the Vital Arts project. Fraser Corfield from ATYP, for example, talked about the 'danger' of programme activities being seen as 'play': 'Because sometimes one of the dangers of what we do is that it's seen as play and therefore while we talk about the skills that are gonna be developed during that, they've always been treated as if they're incidental' (Fraser Corfield, ATYP). This was particularly challenging when justifying programme activities to parents and families. Corfield felt the micro-credentials could provide a useful way of talking about the skills built during programmes in a way that would be more acceptable to families:

> I reckon a whole bunch of parents, if not kids, would jump at that because they want to know that their kids are getting practical skills. You know, the number of phone calls, 'Why are you playing this game? My kid said they just played games all day. What were they doing?' (Fraser Corfield, ATYP)

Corfield was keen to point out that these pressures from parents and families reflected issues of class, culture and access to the arts. Providing evidence of practical skills training through the micro-credentials was a way of increasing access to arts-based activities for young people who may not have the 'time and energy' to engage in arts learning without there being practical outcomes they can evidence. Zoe Scrogings from Corrugated Iron Youth Arts in the Northern Territory echoed this, arguing that providing evidence that programmes were building skills beyond the creative practice was particularly important for First Nations participants.

Conclusion

While digital micro-credentials have long made promises in relation to signalling the skills of young people, and especially young creatives who have learned their skills via informal experience (Mozilla Foundation and Peer 2 Peer University, 2012), we find that a primary involvement in micro-credentials is foremost a form of signalling for the organisations involved in their development. While micro-credentials are understood to signal the skills of participants, of more fundamental importance is how partnership in a project is a way for arts organisations to signal *their* commitment to arts policy. Indeed, fieldwork with young people suggests that 'labour market signalling' is fundamental to the process of developing a micro-credential, even prior to a single badge being issued. 'Signalling' is very much a collective exercise at various levels – involving arts facilitators, directors and academic researchers, as well as youth arts participants, who are keen to signal that they endorse the aims of the project. Overall, the effect is one of sector endorsement of a policy approach – youth arts *should* have employment skills as an outcome; youth arts *does* have employment skills as an outcome. Our finding in this chapter is that the digital micro-credentials embody such declarative statements prior to any badges being issued or skills recognised. This is not to suggest that digital micro-credentials do not or cannot support the recognition of young people's skills, or to question this value claim. Indeed, the project is thoroughly aligned with the educational rationality of youth arts and creative industries policy more broadly (Brook, 2015). It is simply to note that the development of the micro-credentials is, in the first instance, a commitment to this position that is both symbolic and material: the process of developing a digital micro-credential establishes a value claim for youth arts and then translates this into a technical artefact with associated practices.

Technologies produced by promissory discourses are peculiarly sensitive to temporality. They can quickly become dated – abandoned by the actors who may have been insecurely invested – or even abject – examples of a discourse without actors, symbolic gestures heavy with foreknowledge of their own redundancy; or, alternately, timely or on-point, making good on the commitments within the discursive framing; or even dynamic, in so far as the contingencies that were part of their creation inform their design such as to be open to recreation.

FIVE

Practices

Creative practice education teaches and transfers 21st-century skills to young people who engage in youth arts. These soft skills and competencies include creative and critical thinking, empathy, collaboration, social and cultural awareness, belonging and much more. The Vital Arts partnerships with theatre, dance, music and visual arts organisations allowed us to observe the embodied learning that occurs in fieldwork sites, and each of the researchers involved in the project identified and captured evidence of how skills are developed through arts activity. In particular, the youth arts activities of ATYP, The Push, Carclew, Future Foundations and the National Gallery of Victoria (NGV) form a focus of our work here. In this chapter, we also consider the social and cultural diversity of Australian young people in the arts and the diversity of their experiences of arts training and practice. We think through how these experiences inform the development of micro-credentials, and how these micro-credentials can, in turn, give further value and visibility to the skills these young people need to navigate the future landscape of the workplace and, more broadly, a globalised and technologically driven society.

Creative art practices, 21st-century skills and micro-credentials

We take the WEF's definition of 21st-century skills as a framework for observing, analysing and critiquing creative arts practices. We found that the practices in this study were central to informing the development of 21st-century skills, which have been identified as a skills gap internationally by economists and educators. As such, these practices have been integral in the development of the Vital Arts micro-credentials.

As we described in Chapter Three of this book, the WEF 'New vision for education' series (2015, 2016) examines the urgent issue of skills shortages in the evolving technology-centred job market, identifying that an education gap exists between 'minority world' and 'majority world' countries and that each country varies in the level of education in 21st-century skills.[1] In particular, through this series the WEF identifies the skills needed in the 21st century, as shown previously in Figure 3.1.

The three categories of skills, 'foundational literacies', 'competencies' and 'character qualities', are all accompanied, supported and maintained by lifelong learning. The WEF definition of 21st-century skills provided a focus for the Vital Arts research team, as the WEF argues that in today's innovation-driven economy a wider mix of skills are needed. As well as requiring *foundational literacies*, young people need the *competencies* of critical thinking/problem solving, creativity, communication and collaboration and *character qualities* of curiosity, initiative, persistence/grit, adaptability, leadership and social and cultural awareness. Skills taught in the youth art sector can hone these skills further, particularly when looking at *competencies* and *character qualities*.

The WEF report argues that as continued technological progress increases, automated processes will replace human labour, and the job market will move further away from routine manual labour and more towards non-routine jobs which require analytical thinking and interpersonal skills. As such, these so-called 21st-century skills will be increasingly required in the future. In economies more reliant on innovation, skilled jobs will become wholly dependent on creativity, problem solving and collaboration as a way of solving unstructured problems and effectively analysing information.

However, as we argued in Chapter Three, skills taxonomies such as those presented by the WEF often ignore the 'social life' of skills and their development. Vital Arts positions these competencies and character qualities as skills acquired through the sustained practice of various art forms, where artists undertake training to continually develop their creative thinking and solve problems for specific contexts. In this way, we recontextualise 21st-century skills and their development within the youth arts context. The research positions these skills, acquired through arts training, as valuable for our future society and as a way to contribute to changing the perception of arts training as 'art for art's sake' (a 19th-century European attitude that art is developed purely for the sake of inner development, assuming this can be separated from a greater social good). This social attitude has often left the arts sector in a marginalised state of vulnerable employment status rather than the source of practices which contribute to broader society and potentially train young people for varied careers. Through observing the work of our youth arts partners and developing detailed understandings of the nature of arts training, we have documented how the skills taught and practised as part of arts work lead to developing the competencies and character qualities sought after for future innovation economy-based employability.

Learning to be 'creative' in an innovation-based economy

'Creativity' is a valuable skill in the 21st-century workforce and is recognised and developed exceptionally well in art education. However, where in Chapter Three we demonstrated that 'creativity' has been positioned as critical to an innovation-based economy, particularly as a means to identify and extract value, educators have long viewed creative skills as some of the more complex to achieve. The educational framework 'Taxonomy of educational objectives' (Bloom et al, 1956) (also known as 'Bloom's taxonomy') categorises educational goals and is used by many generations of educational staff. The aim of the taxonomy was to support educators and learners to establish learning goals. 'Create' is defined as 'produce new or original work – design, assemble, construct, conjecture, develop, formulate, author or investigate' and sits at the top of the pyramid in the taxonomy, as it involves the many skills needed to achieve this type of thought process. 'Bloom's taxonomy' demonstrates the many layers of cognitive skills development required to reach a creative state. This includes not only being able to apply skills but also analyse and evaluate a situation, skills also recognised as 21st-century competencies under the framework of 'critical thinking/problem solving'.

The original taxonomy was developed in 1956 by Benjamin Bloom with collaborators Max Englehart, Edward Furst, Walter Hill and David Krathwohl. The earlier version positions knowledge as the highest-order skill, defined as involving 'the recall of specifics and universals, the recall of methods and processes, or the recall of a pattern, structure, or setting'. As society has evolved and technological advances are able to support learners with the recall of information, methods and processes, the taxonomy was revised and renamed 'A taxonomy for teaching, learning and assessing' (Anderson and Krathwohl, 2001) by cognitive psychologists, curriculum theorists and instructional researchers to move away from the static notion of educational objectives towards a more dynamic and active framing of these skills, as demonstrated in Figure 5.1. This positioned 'create' as a skill that requires the many former levels of skills to be able to achieve creative abilities.

We witnessed these key stages in remembering and understanding, applying, analysing and evaluating but also found that arts settings have a high percentage of neurodivergent

Figure 5.1: Bloom's taxonomy

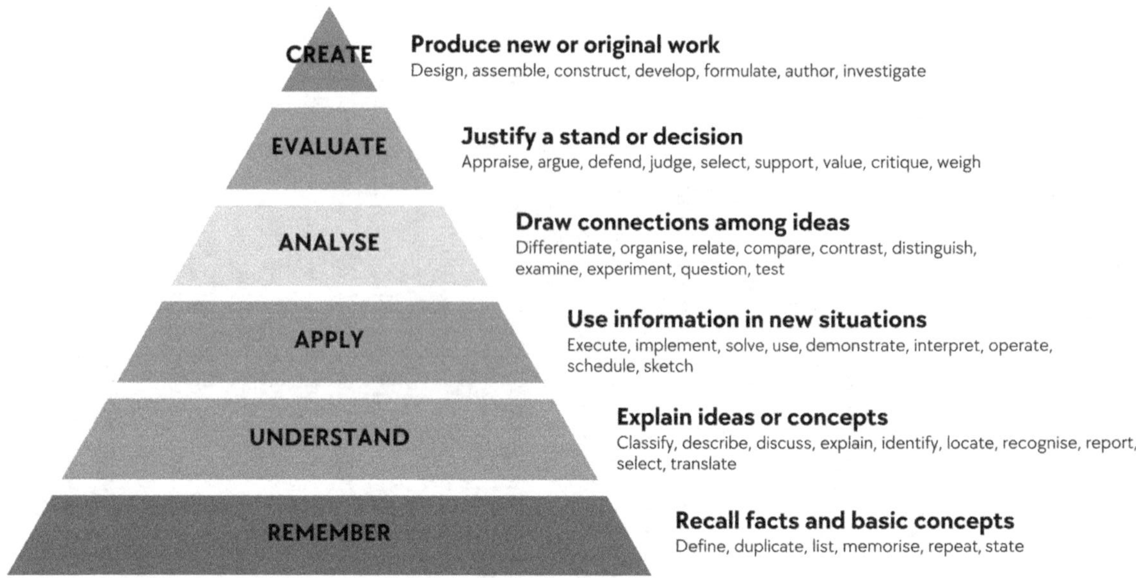

Source: Bloom's revised taxonomy, diagram based on original work of Armstrong (2010): Vanderbilt University Center for Teaching

young people who do not process learning experiences as Bloom presents. From a neurodivergent perspective, there are several problems with Bloom's taxonomy that become visible around its hierarchies, rigid categories and assumptions about cognition. Bloom frames learning as a ladder, and the stairs on that ladder are to: remember, understand, apply, analyse, evaluate, create. For many neurodivergent learners (those with autism, attention deficit hyperactivity disorder [ADHD], dyslexia and so on), cognition doesn't follow this linear progression. For example, an autistic student might jump straight to analysis or creative synthesis without being able to 'recall' rote facts. An ADHD student may generate and create before fully 'understanding' in Bloom's terms, because ideation often precedes structured comprehension. This means the taxonomy can pathologise non-linear learning as a deficit rather than recognising it as valid. From a neurodivergent perspective, the divides between cognitive, affective and psychomotor domains that Bloom develops are artificial. Bloom compartmentalises learning into separate 'domains'; however, neurodivergent learners often experience thinking as multi-sensory and affectively entangled: emotions, bodily sensations and cognition are inseparable. For example, sensory overwhelm or hyperfocus profoundly shape the way memory and understanding unfold. Bloom's taxonomy's rigid separation ignores how feeling, movement, memory and thought interweave in neurodivergent processing. In an innovation-based economy, which relies on the human capital of creative thinking to solve contemporary problems, the development of creative thinking skills is necessary, and we can point to arts education as a way of building young people's capacity in creative skills.

Research in youth arts settings

Between 2001 and 2005, we observed existing activities of our youth arts partner organisations over extended periods of time and undertook interviews and group discussions with young participants and staff. This allowed us to observe how these activities build 21st-century skill competencies, and we have used these findings to inform the development of our micro-credentials. We have considered how young people engage in arts activities in a process of embodied and tacit learning, where learning occurs through the entire body and relies on the various senses to assess the situation and make judgements in order to solve problems. Three of our partners, including ATYP (a non-profit theatre arts organisation dedicated to young people), The Push (a non-profit contemporary music organisation for youth) and ACMI will be discussed later in this chapter. Our other substantial engagements with the CMY, the NGV Ambassadors programme, Future Foundations and Carclew Youth Arts are discussed in other chapters of this book.

Our industry partners were framed as sites of action research, as an 'action research' methodology focuses on the study of everyday contexts and their communities (in this case youth arts organisations and their activities) to understand and analyse the specific context and to find effective solutions together through a combination of professional and community practices. In *Action Research* (2014), educator Ernest T. Stringer states that

> [a]ction research is a systematic approach to investigation that enables people to find effective solutions to problems they confront in their everyday lives … In doing so it also seeks to build a body of knowledge that enhances professional and community practices and works to increase the well-being of the people involved. (2014: 277)

By taking part in the activities of industry members and activities during our fieldwork, we were able to observe and witness the building of a community around a body of knowledge specific to an art form.

We also gained an understanding of how young people were supported to develop these skills, not only through the practice of the art form but also by mentors and collaborators to learn as a community. An action research approach allows us to consider the various stakeholders involved and how these partners have an impact on the development of 21st-century skills through teaching a particular art form: 'Action research is based on localised studies that focus on the need to understand how things are happening, rather than merely on what is happening, and to understand the ways that stakeholders – people concerned with the issue – perceive, interpret and respond to events related to the issue investigated' (Stringer, 2014: 36).

By understanding this more wholistic approach to learning through an art form in the fieldwork sites, we were able to gain an understanding of the processes of training in the arts and how this can lead to the practice and strengthening of creative thinking, critical thinking and collaborative skills, which are highly sought after and highly transferable to contexts beyond the arts in an innovation-based economy.

What is 'creative art practice'?

Creative skills are less mysterious than some might suggest. The continued practice of foundational skills is key. It is not allusive; it is practice. During the process of developing our micro-credentials to recognise 21st-century skills, we worked with our partners to consider what 'creative art practices' are for each of their art forms and, in turn, how we will engage with these activities in the design of our micro-creds. We wanted to recognise that it is during this process of being engaged in 'creative arts practice' that learning to apply these physical core skills occurs concurrently with the development of 21st-century cognitive competencies and character qualities.

The term 'creative' can be defined as 'inventive and imaginative', and 'art' as 'human creative skill or its application'

(Moore, 2004). With these definitions in mind, our partners were selected as important contributors to this research, as they are defined by the ability to be inventive and imaginative in teaching and cultivating skills in their specialised art forms of theatre, dance, music and the visual arts.

The term 'practice' has a few definitions, including 'perform habitually; carry out in action: practice the same method', and it can imply that performing an activity habitually can improve skills, particularly when defined as 'do repeatedly as an exercise to improve a skill'. More so, 'practice' can further imply it is possible to become 'experienced, expert, skilful through much practice', that it is possible to master a skill, in this case to master a creative art practice. Through our fieldwork, we observed that each of our partners had a community of dedicated practitioners, both professionals and learners, at various levels, facilities and environments conducive to the development of skills specific to their art form discipline.

Creative arts practice is an embodied type of learning, where thinking occurs with physical skills and activities. In 'Thinking through practice', Duxbury et al (2008: 7) unpack what it means to think through creative practice, where the process of repeatedly engaging and mastering skills is sustained through enquiry, which requires creative practitioners to question, review, reflect, analyse, perform, speculate, relate, remember, critique, construct and ultimately further question to create something new (skills which are reflected in Bloom's revised taxonomy, 'A taxonomy for teaching, learning and assessing' [Anderson and Krathwohl, 2001]). It is a marriage between the actions of the body and the ability to express thoughts and ideas through the body. This creates a unique type of learning that builds the skills needed in a future society.

The arts and embodied learning: mind–body dualism vs mindfulness

The embodied learning that occurs in youth arts settings is a natural state of learning that requires engagement and coordination from the whole physical body, the senses, the emotions and processes of the mind. Put simply, our bodies are hardwired to move and be active. In the Western education system, which continues to be influential in our globalised environment, emphasis has traditionally been placed on the capacity of cultivating knowledge (as demonstrated by Bloom's original taxonomy [Bloom et al 1956]) and the mind, leading to the idea of 'mind–body dualism', where the mind and body are conceptualised as two different unrelated forms, a concept which can be traced back to René Descartes' *Meditations for First Philosophy* (1641).

Although we have come a long way from this, the legacy of this approach is still evident through the dominance of sitting in educational environments. Contemporary educators have often critiqued this approach as having limitations, with more recent literature and practices in education supporting a more connected and embodied approach to learning, especially in young people. Susan Hrach's *Minding Bodies* (2021) addresses this very issue of learning which occurs through the whole body by learning skills through physical movement, attention to the spatial environment and providing sensory experiences. Buddhist monk, educator and peace activist Thich Nhat Hanh (1926–2022), known as the 'Father of Mindfulness', also advocates for reuniting the mind and body as one, stating that continuing to see the mind and body as separate entities is creating wider social problems: 'We think that there's something wrong with our minds or something wrong with our bodies, and that we need to fix or heal that one, separate thing. But it's impossible to remove mind from body or body from mind. They are two manifestations of the same thing' (Nhat Hanh, 2014: 10). Arts education is an embodied approach to learning which can have much further reaching implications in the development of the critical skills needed in the skills gap shortage.

An embodied approach shows us that knowledge can be embedded as corporeal knowledge, knowledge that can be gained through the practising of physical bodily action. In considering the way artists use their body in practice to develop a body of knowledge, 'artists embody their art practice due to repetition of movement, familiarity with tools and increased confidence in the nature of their practice' (Budge, 2016). Through the building of creative skills with the support of tools, a practising artist gains a high level of skill and confidence, and the application of these skills creatively contributes to expanding their creative thinking capacity. When a particular level of skill is obtained by a creative practitioner, these are skills which can be enacted without the process of thinking through each of the stages – the activity becomes automatic, without the practitioner being conscious of the many layers of mental processes that are required.

This is often referred to as a 'flow state', identified by psychologist Mihaly Csikszentmihalyi in *Flow: The Psychology of Optimal Experience* (1991). Flow was first observed in artists who were completely focused on the act of creative production. While flow was first identified and studied in artists, Csikszentmihalyi acknowledges it is a creative state not exclusive to artists but can be witnessed in all individuals engaged in focused creative time. Flow is considered a state of mind when there is conscious harmony and order in the enacting of an activity, intense attention is focused on a goal that matches the skills in action and everything else is forgotten in that moment. For example, when a dancer learns a new routine, they may at first be unfamiliar with the movements, the timing, the spatial positioning of their body, but after spending the time to concentrate on specific movements through imitation, they soon learn to move their body as witnessed. With practice, these moves become familiar and, eventually with enough training, automatic, thus developing into the mindful action of a flow state.

Relating back to the way the foundational skills may transpire and build 21st-century skills, practitioners may start to confidently consider alternative ways to apply their skills. As they build their library of skills, they learn to use these foundational skills and their confidence, and they may consider how they might alter or bring to these skills their own individual interpretation and thus start to develop their creative thinking abilities. Once asked to consider the specific context of the performance they are engaged with, they take those creative thinking skills and apply them to context, therefore exercising their critical thinking and problem-solving skills. A further sharing of the approach they are taking requires the communication of their individual interpretation, thus leading to the potential of collaboration through the act of sharing.

Fieldwork: building a community of creative practice

The youth arts organisations chosen for this research project include arts organisations in a diversity of art forms including theatre, music, dance and the visual arts. Different specific physical and practical skills are required to learn and innovate in all of these art forms. Organisations which focus on establishing the skills and competencies required to practise an art form become sites of learning, where a community of practitioners can gather to understand, engage and practise together. It is a safe community and place where individuals can develop their skills, practise, fail and succeed and be pushed to challenge themselves further with the support of arts educators – a space necessary for the development of an individual practice that may contribute to the individual's potential and wider culture of the art form.

In *The Element* (Robinson and Aronica, 2009), Robinson proposes that when creative talents meet their passion for an art form, they are able to reach their full potential. It is not only their talents, skills and passion that are important but also the process of connecting with other people with shared interests. In doing so, creatives develop a community or network of peers and cultivate a culture of learners around the art form. This is why young people finding an arts organisation dedicated to building skills in a particular art form is valuable. In doing so they build a sub-culture of practice, which they may not be able to nurture in the mainstream school system.

Fieldwork study: ATYP

> The rehearsal room shifts when the intimacy coordinator steps in: everything becomes more precise. The air tightens around intention. What had, moments before, been loose improvisation now becomes structured attention.
>
> 'Again', she says, not to demand repetition, but to locate clarity.
>
> They are working on a sequence of ultraviolence drawn from *A Clockwork Orange*, a scene that, in narrative terms, is chaotic, impulsive, excessive. But here, in rehearsal, nothing is left to impulse. One of the young actors playing a Droog steps forward, then pauses.
>
> 'Can we mark the contact points?' he asks.
>
> There is no bravado in the question. Only care.
>
> They gather in a small cluster, mapping the scene verbally before moving. Shoulder, forearm, rib: not as sites of impact, but as coordinates in a shared choreography. The intimacy coordinator guides the conversation, reframing 'hits' as offers and responses. Violence becomes a sequence of cues, each dependent on mutual recognition. 'Your hand stops here', she demonstrates, hovering just short of another actor's chest. 'The illusion happens because he moves, not because you strike.'
>
> They try it
>
> A swing, stopped in air. A body recoils: precisely timed. A thud, created not through contact, but through a foot stamping the floor in synchrony. The sound arrives as if it belongs to the body, though it does not. From the outside, it reads as aggression. Inside the sequence, it feels like listening. What becomes visible, slowly, is a different kind of masculinity at work.

These young men, tasked with embodying menace, move with acute sensitivity to one another. Eyes track micro-signals. Breathing synchronises. A missed cue is not pushed through; it is reset.

'Hold', someone says mid-run.

They stop instantly.

'Your timing was early', another actor offers, not as critique, but as calibration. 'I didn't have space to respond.'

They walk it back. Try again.

There is a kind of intimacy here that sits in tension with the content they are producing. The scene demands domination, unpredictability, threat. The rehearsal produces predictability, trust. At one point, the actor playing Alex experiments with a more forceful gesture: a faster swing, closer to the body.

The intimacy coordinator intervenes immediately.

'Let's not escalate speed before we stabilise the pattern', she says. 'Control first. Then intensity.'

He nods, steps back, resets.

What is striking is not the correction, but the ease with which it is absorbed. Authority circulates differently here. It is not imposed; it is distributed across the ensemble, anchored in a shared commitment to safety and precision.

They begin layering sound.

A low chant emerges – rhythmic, almost percussive. It echoes the sonic textures of the production, reminiscent of the charged atmosphere surrounding A Clockwork Orange, but reworked through the bodies in the room.

The choreography tightens.

Step. Swing. Recoil. Stamp.

Each action is both individual and collective. The illusion of chaos is built from an underlying grid of agreement.

During a break, one actor flexes his wrist, another rolls out his shoulders. They check in with each other – not performatively, but habitually.

'You good?'

'Yeah. You?'

'Yeah.'

It is a simple exchange, but it carries weight. Consent here is not a one-time negotiation; it is ongoing, iterative, embedded in the rhythm of rehearsal.

When they run the full sequence, something shifts again.

The violence lands, not as real harm, but as convincing representation. The audience, when it comes, will see menace, volatility, the dangerous charisma of youth. What they will not see is the infrastructure beneath it: the careful spacing, the negotiated timing, the constant micro-adjustments that make the scene possible.

From the edge of the room, it becomes clear that what is being trained is not just performance, but a form of relational intelligence.

The young men are not simply learning how to enact violence.

They are learning how to withhold it, how to simulate it without reproducing harm, how to remain accountable to one another even while portraying its absence.

'Once more', the coordinator says.

They reset, take their positions.

And again, the choreography unfolds: precise, controlled, collaborative.

Ultraviolence, rendered through care.

The project in development

In July 2022, Anna and Tammy attended rehearsal sessions for a professional production of *A Clockwork Orange: A Play with Music* (1987) with young actors from ATYP as fieldwork researchers (ATYP, 2022). ATYP is a nationally and globally recognised theatre company that champions young artists and is based in Sydney's Walsh Bay. They produce and train young people in the theatre arts (such as acting, writing and producing) and develop professional productions focusing on innovation, artistic excellence and collaboration.

Written by Anthony Burgess, *A Clockwork Orange: A Play with Music* is an adaption of his original novella (1962) and was produced after director Stanley Kubrick's famous film version in 1971. It tells the provocative story of youth male culture, enacting violence and the consequences for individual, society and the state. The main character Alex and his gang, the Droogs, spend their drug-fuelled nights embarking on ultraviolence. Afterwards, Alex is jailed for a violent crime and must submit to behaviour-modification techniques to gain his freedom. Returning to society, he becomes a victim of those he terrorised in the past. The play continues to appeal to audiences as it tackles the timeless themes and questions of free will, adolescence, the human capacity for violence and the power of the state.

The young actors were all professionally trained in tertiary education courses and had auditioned and successfully been cast in the roles in this professional production. During our time there, we witnessed the actors working with a variety of professional staff including experienced actors, choreographers for movement and stunts, music and sound directors and stage designers. In a few days, we observed the many multidisciplinary activities they took part in to prepare to perform the play live. As researchers, the crew even asked us to take part in warm-up activities, which involved gentle Tai Chi Chuan exercises and warming up our vocal cords by creating sounds with our voices. This gave us a taste of the embodied experience of taking part in the arts. Through witnessing (and participating in) the young actors' activities, we witnessed a demonstration of collaborative and creative and critical problem-solving skills enacted through their daily practice.

Physical movement and embodying representations of youth

The actors learned to use their bodies as musical instruments, creating thumping sounds in coordination with their movements to present as though they were really involved in a fight. In portraying the scene of menacing violent teenage characters, the actors embarked on training and practising the act of street fighting, which was supported by a choreographer. The actors prepared by discussing and analysing the characters they were playing as a group. They then considered how they would use their body language to portray the culture of menacing young adolescents. These sessions were often physically gruelling, with the actors repeatedly working hard with their bodies during these sessions.

The actors also worked closely with a music director, who worked with the young actors on the musical parts of the production. This involved warming up and practising projecting their voices in particular ways suitable for the telling of the story being portrayed. Using song to create a menacing tone for a scene where violence was to be enacted led to sounds being created that replicated the intimidating sound of male football chanting. The actors and their trainers discussed the sound they were trying to recreate for the scene at great length, working through issues of volume and rhythm, which would help audiences to experience the scene as tense and filled with the potential of masculine aggression. The discussion involved the critiquing of the sounds they were making and whether or not it was the right sound to express the mood of the scene, which required a nuanced understanding of the subculture the young actors were imitating in order to analyse and critique the scenario they were portraying.

The script and critical discussion

Through discussing and analysing the script, the dialogue often led to a deeper understanding of the social and cultural contexts of the scenes. After a long morning of physical work, the actors worked on their scripts, reading through their lines together, analysing each line, considering the emotional quality and working through the relationships between the characters being portrayed. A further challenge of the script was the use of 'Nadsat', an imagined hybrid language of Russian and English, which contained rhyming slang. A big part of the experience was not only uncoding the language but also learning how to interpret the text in a way that was suitable for the characters being portrayed. This experience certainly built the cross-cultural capacities of the actors by having to imagine and demonstrate a hybrid language.

Designing the space for the actors

We also witnessed conversations between the set designer, the actors and directors, where they discussed what was required for the production. Based on these conversations, the set designer developed set designs and represented these ideas to the group. During this representation, the group critiqued what would be most appropriate and how they would function within the space, with the dialogue together becoming a collaborative activity.

Collaborating with the team

Throughout the process, strong communication skills and group coordination were required, as the actors needed to train and practise together supported by older experienced mentors. It required a high level of being able to read each other's movements and being able to collaborate on scenarios under development. All the actors exhibited an understanding of working towards a shared goal of performing the scene to their best ability.

Reflection of ATYP

Each of the actors were required to demonstrate character qualities of *curiosity*, *initiative*, *persistence/grit*, *adaptability* and *leadership* as they worked through the different sequences of the production. In particular, the competency of *critical thinking/problem solving* was observed in many of the activities, particularly in the analysis and critiquing of the script and resolving how the actors portrayed the characters to represent their emotional quality and the narrative being presented. The actors used their *creativity* through the way they uniquely interpreted the material in their performances. Working as a team, the actors had to demonstrate clear *communication* throughout their rehearsals to ensure they were working *collaboratively* and in coordination with each other. The nuanced discussions that occurred between the actors about cultural and sub-cultural social norms in the context of the play certainly developed their understanding of *social and cultural awareness*.

Fieldwork study: ACMI and Film It

The Vital Arts programme also engaged with members of ACMI's education team through the advisory Action Research Industry Group. ACMI, the national museum of screen culture in Australia, runs a variety of education programmes for young people and students to learn skills across film, television and game production. Film It, for example, is an intensive one-day programme for school-aged students that allows students to interpret and film a screenplay. Students are provided with a script at the start of the day and, in groups, begin the work of interpreting the script, developing a storyboard to map out the camera shots and then film and edit the screenplay. The finished works are then played for their peers for critical reflection.

Throughout research interviews, the ACMI education team identified a number of ways that the Film It programme, among other education programmes at ACMI, developed critical skills and competencies in young people.

Skills development through Film It

> [T]he kids have to move very fast throughout the day and they've got to adapt to the different requirements of what it is that they're creating. So they're thinking on their feet quite a lot. (Christine Evely, ACMI)

Upon receiving their script, the students are asked to interpret the film, breaking up into groups and using pens and pencils to mark up the script and draw out ideas about genre, visual interpretation through camera shots, characters, props and so on. They then use this initial work to create a storyboard and eventually film their production. Through each of these stages, the students are encouraged to think critically about how their interpretation of the script can be explored and realised through their film production. Throughout the day, they have to consider how to use the grounds around ACMI as a film site, use the materials around them as props and develop their characters as actors in the scene. The students are also encouraged to critically interrogate and play with genre, thinking about how certain tropes can uphold or subvert audience expectations. As described in the previous excerpt by the head of education at ACMI, Christine Evely, this intense process of filming in a short amount of time requires the students to be highly adaptable. As they move through different roles and encounter different obstacles and challenges, they need to work together to realise their final production.

The Film It programme encourages the kind of embodied learning described earlier in this chapter. Here, students are taking the words off the page and into the spatial environment. The students move from interpreting the script, to creating a storyboard, to filming and finally editing their scene. At each stage, they are engaging in acts of negotiation in order to realise their vision. For the staff at ACMI, the programme acts as a space to draw out leadership potential and empower young people:

> We often get teachers commenting after our programmes that kids who don't normally speak up will speak up in our programmes, and we often get comments that someone who might be a bit of a challenge in the classroom is actually really shining in a programme like this because they're getting a chance to do something that's quite different to the way they learn in a school environment. (Christine Evely, ACMI)

Evely's comments here demonstrate the complex role these programmes play in 'youth empowerment'. As Evely's comments make clear, creative programmes often act as instruments of governance, aimed at solving the *problem* of young people who are 'a challenge' in traditional classroom settings. Simultaneously, however, the programmes are genuine sites of creative expression for these young people. Garry Westmore, the producer of the schools programme at ACMI, described it as 'a little bit of creative chaos'. It is in this space of creative chaos that young people are developing skills, enacting their own agency and negotiating their place in the future of work. The creative chaos that Westmore describes also helps to move the young person from a state of governability to ungovernability. In this way, the creative space allows traditional boundaries and knowledge of the self to be explored and extended, experienced by teachers and the programme staff as the students 'really shining' to use Evely's words (Clammer, 2023). As Adams describes in a discussion of Theatre of the Oppressed in-school programmes, youth arts facilitators are often caught between insider and outsider positionalities (Adams, 2019: 326). As outsiders, arts facilitators can help subvert systems of power and oppression that might be found in traditional educational systems; however, simultaneously these workers often have to position themselves as insiders in order to gain access to these school sites, problematising their ability to disrupt these power dynamics. Thus youth arts programmes can become ambiguous sites of youth governability, where questions of power and agency can be articulated, explored and played with between facilitators and participants.

While Film It is ostensibly designed to develop specific vocational skills in film making, through the programme, students embark on a broader journey of *skills discovery*. Through the creative practice of film making, the students likewise begin to embody skills such as problem solving, critical thinking, teamwork, leadership and creativity. Short programmes such as Film It help students to push back against the 'lack' or 'deficit' discourse permeating policy arenas, where young people are continually positioned as lacking skills for the workforce and their futures. Instead, the way that young people perform certain skills through the creative practice of these one-day programmes demonstrates how the skills were already in development within the young person, and they simply needed to be given the space and guidance to practise them. The idea of practice itself necessarily belies the deficit discourse. A skill is not something that somebody either has or does not have but instead can always be acquired, developed and honed through use. By bringing these skills out and providing that opportunity to practise, these programmes therefore support young people to view themselves as skilled, agentive and already 'employable'.

Fieldwork study: The Push and FReeZA All-Ages Tour

The Push is a Melbourne-based youth music organisation in Australia that aims to give young people access to music programmes and events. The All-Ages Tour, delivered through the FReeZA programme, trains and supports committees of young people to stage large all-ages music events in their local communities. Usually supported by a local government youth worker, these committees are responsible for staging the live music events over a six- to eight-month period. This includes tasks such as finding venues, booking and coordinating local artists to perform, marketing the event and coordination on the day of the event. The Push helps to provide training and support to these committees of young people to ensure they have the skills and know-how necessary to stage the event. While The Push provides this training, according to CEO Kate Duncan, much of the learning happens on the job: 'It's all through that real life on the job experience that they learn.' Across the six to eight months that the programme runs, participants have ample opportunity to practise and develop a range of skills.

The ethos of The Push is often focused on access – how young people can have greater access not just to live music events in their area but also to the skills and know-how to stage these events. One of the young research participants who was involved in producing a live music tour with The Push talked extensively about the skills and know-how they developed through their participation. They talked about coordinating artists and backstage staff, scheduling activities, tracking finances, navigating local noise laws and Environmental Protection Authority compliance, organising travel, marketing, running end-of-show evaluations, managing conflict and so on. As the participant spent more time on tour, their confidence in their own skills grew, particularly as greater trust was placed in them to coordinate and manage specific tasks. They talked about 'moving past' limiting mindsets about their abilities, realising that they can 'do this' and becoming 'more and more comfortable' with certain tasks: 'I've broadened my technical knowledge, developed my interpersonal skills particularly the ability to be adaptable and think on my feet and my confidence has skyrocketed' (research participant).

This kind of skills development has obvious benefits for the young participant but likewise ensures that industry know-how is being passed on to a new generation, keeping the industry alive and ensuring continued access for future generations. In this way, practice is not just an individual pursuit but a collective one. Passing on practices helps to sustain subcultures, identities and scenes. This is not just about the individual employability of a young person but sustaining and nurturing collective cultural capacities.

Conclusion

To conclude, this chapter has considered how 21st-century skills can be acquired through the embodied learning of youth arts education, as demonstrated through ATYP, ACMI and The Push case studies. In addition to these case studies, these skills were also found in other fieldwork sites for the Vital Arts project, including organisations such as Carclew, Future Foundations and the NGV Ambassadors programme. The training and continued practice of youth arts has the potential to build foundational embodied skills and concurrently lead to the building and enhancing of cognitive competencies and character qualities, identified as a skills shortage in today's innovation economy. Arts training must be further recognised and valued as fundamental education to build 21st-century skills in young people and for the social good. It is a key reason why developing a 21st-century skills micro-credential course learnt through arts participation is necessary and potentially widens participation in gaining these skills. Particularly, as a tool, micro-credentials can help to accredit and recognise the practice-based learning that is already occurring in these youth arts spaces. In doing so, skills become recontextualised as sites of struggle and negotiation, where the agency of young people is paramount. In this way, the micro-credentials can help to bridge the gap between the abstract identification of 21st-century skills required for the new work order and the social life of these skills as embodied and developed in specific youth arts contexts.

SIX

Diverse economies

Diversity cred and racialised young people in the creative industries

In this chapter, we draw on our empirical research to explore ways that workplaces are reckoning with economies of cultural and racial diversity. The WEF reports on diversity and inclusion policies and the extent to which they support equity or undermine meritocracies (Jha, 2023). The International Labour Organization (ILO) frames diversity as a resource, stating that highly diverse and inclusive workplaces are 'associated with greater productivity, innovation and workforce well-being' (ILO, 2022). The business management discourse of 'cultural intelligence' offers a similarly optimistic analysis: diversity is something that can be leveraged through various kinds of cognitive capacities and practical strategies (Livermore, 2009). The dominant discourse here suggests that if managed successfully, a culturally diverse workforce is key to unlocking business opportunities in the global marketplace. However, these buoyant approaches overlook the ways race, gender and class differences complicate the productivity agenda and how human diversity disrupts the mobilisation of human capital.

This chapter asks how diversity is, or can be, understood within the framework of '21st-century skills' and what this skills agenda has to offer racialised young people. It considers whether the kinds of cultural knowledge and competencies these young people bring can be framed as 'skills' in the context of new formations of value and continuing dynamics of racialised exclusion in the 21st-century workplace. The first half of this chapter explores how racial and cultural difference, and questions of inclusion/exclusion, are reflected in the skills discourse. It asks whether competencies such as 'social and cultural awareness' and 'cultural and civic literacy' can be more than commodities or instruments for supporting business objectives and whether they can be enlisted in critical projects of inclusion or anti-racism.

The second half of the chapter explores how these categories operate in practice, through a study of the CMY Culture Spring programme as an example of how racially diverse young people respond to the kinds of 'cred' a career in the creative industries demands. As a general idea, 'youth cred' merges different definitions of 'culture': as the norms and practices emerging from a 'way of life' (Williams, 1961); as forms of 'capital' tied to aesthetic, subcultural or formal systems of knowledge (Bourdieu, 1986); and as an anthropological position related to race and ethnicity (Ang, 2001). Young people's ability to leverage these kinds of 'culture' shape their opportunities for participation in creative spaces: in art galleries, music programmes and so on. If micro-credentials are an instrument for recognising young people's skills acquired through creative participation, this chapter examines how creative contexts also come with their own systems of credibility and legitimation. There is a need to understand how these systems are being shaped by diversity politics, and how shifting formulations of youth 'cred' are converging with what we describe as 'diversity cred'.

Diversity cred is a 'regime of value' (Appadurai, 1988) in the creative industries, emerging from a business imperative to engage with multicultural and transnational markets and from a more general aspiration to signal good organisational citizenship. It describes the repurposing of a positive orientation towards cultural diversity as a strategic economic and cultural resource. Industry desire to demonstrate diversity cred presents non-white young people, whose cultural identities and knowledge become reframed as assets, with new professional opportunities. This chapter presents data from a study of young, non-white interns at a global media company seeking to consolidate diversity cred as part of its own value proposition. We explore how these efforts involve new ways of valuing non-white young people, at the same time as it leaves in place old structures of non-belonging.

This chapter examines how diversity functions in two ways. The first is as a strategy of value creation within the creative industries. The second is as a critique of dominant visions of young people's education and employment pathways, in the context of a settler-colonial, 'white nation' (Hage, 1998). Although the category of race as a basis of biological differentiation has been 'thoroughly discredited' (Hesmondhalgh and Saha, 2013: 180), migrant and Indigenous young people in Australia – who make up around half of the country's young people – continue to be racialised and minoritised in spaces of work, education, the arts and leisure (Wyn et al, 2018). It is vital that youth researchers attend to these processes of racialisation and contest the supposed neutrality of frameworks that manage young people's experiences. This chapter supports Idriss et al's call for a 'race critical analysis' of youth studies concepts (Idriss et al, 2022). Among these, they suggest, are 'youth transitions', an idea that centres the experience of the white youthful subject and benchmarks of independence and mobility that do not apply to all young people; and 'the enterprising self', which similarly deploys culturally specific understandings of how young people internalise conditions of precarity, risk and opportunity (Idriss et al, 2022). While this chapter does not offer a sustained analysis of these concepts, it shows how young people's creative and vocational participation involves a range of career aspirations, modes of citizenship and standards of credibility that are shaped by their experiences of race.

The chapter argues that while the concept of '21st-century skills' promises inclusion, it can also be a universalising discourse. The framework's emphasis on 'social and cultural awareness' presents a normative vision of what the 21st-century workplace should look like, and of the value of 'culture'. However, in this skills schema, all culture and all bodies are equal, and there is no way of valuing the particular cultural competencies and knowledge (which includes knowledge about inequality and racism) that racialised young people bring. It is suggested that non-white young people experience exclusion in the creative industries even while being valued for their cultural literacy and 'diversity cred'. At the same time, their inclusion in the kind of work explored here can support the development of creativity, persistence, adaptability and initiative and, in doing so, could enable fuller participation in these industries. A micro-credential instrument that is attentive to these modes of learning could support these participation goals and also make visible the critical, contextual skills needed for diverse young people to endure, and intervene, in exclusionary workplaces.

Locating 'culture' within 21st-century skills

The 21st-century skills framework is a potentially useful tool for young people looking to communicate the competencies and embodied knowledge they have cultivated through creative participation. Such uses challenge critiques of micro-credentials as an overly narrow and technocratic instrument that decontextualises knowledge from its cultural contexts (Wheelahan and Moodie, 2022). This application of the skills framework is also worth considering in relation to critiques that it lacks a normative agenda. It has been argued, for example, that the 21st-century skills discourse offers an 'essentially neutral' set of prescriptions, 'lacking meaningful reference to content, direction and larger purpose' (Howard, 2018: 188). Such concerns reflect a desire to move beyond the rationalist and functional aim of preparing learners for a globalised knowledge economy to a more humanistic vision of the purpose of education. However, others argue that the skills discourse can be read more expansively, as containing a values-driven citizenship agenda. It has been suggested that the particular ways of learning, thinking, working and living in the world promoted by the framework might even be redefined as '21st-century values' rather than 'skills' (Kennedy et al, 2022). This confluence between skills and values emerges from a longer history of citizenship education that connects 'broad knowledge' and 'critical thinking' with the cultivation of 'moral and civil character' (Jung, 2016: 5). These connections explain why recent iterations of 21st-century skills combine technical competencies with character dispositions and qualities.

'Culture' plays an important role in this humanistic project. In the late 20th century, the historical idea of the well-rounded citizen who should use their knowledge to 'improve the world' (Jung, 2016: 5), was updated to respond to globalisation and increased cultural diversity. Rizvi and Choo's description of global citizenship education demonstrates how the citizenship agenda deploys culture by encompassing 'international mindedness' and 'intercultural understanding' (2020: 2). 'Skills' instruments have responded by incorporating such competencies and addressing an economic landscape understood to be fraught with complexity, uncertainty and instability and shaped by evolving digital technologies (Shliakhovchuk, 2021; Australian Government, 2022). 'Culture' appears in these frameworks in the form of 'cultural and civic literacy', or via the 'character quality' of 'social and cultural awareness' (WEF, 2015). The Australian government highlights 'intercultural understanding' as part of its wider framework of 21st-century learning that organises skills into 'ways of thinking', 'ways of working', 'tools for working' and 'living in the world' (Australian Government, 2022). 'Living in the world' includes 'citizenship – local and global' and 'personal and social responsibility – including cultural awareness and competence' (Australian Government, 2022).

These policies highlight how global citizenship education ideals overlap with the commodification of cultural competencies emphasised in business management discourse. Shliakhovchuk (2021) usefully reflects on how 'cultural literacy', an idea that originated in the 1940s, has come to be championed by both governmental institutions like the United Nations Educational, Scientific and Cultural Organization and corporations like Google. Writing about the US context, she traces how evolving definitions of literacy respond to shifting societal demands, from the post-war ideal of 'tolerance towards others', to the idea of 'cultural capital' and the ability to 'engage fully' in a given culture through an understanding of its signs, symbols, language and stories (Shliakhovchuk, 2021: 231). More broadly, Shliakhovchuk describes how cultural literacy has come to involve a critical reflexiveness and self-awareness towards one's culture, as well as intercultural communication skills. The term gave rise to the idea of 'intercultural literacy' and the more business-oriented 'cultural intelligence' or 'CQ' in the early 2000s (Earley and Ang, 2003; Livermore, 2009). These constructs reflect the dual function of cultural literacy, to both 'comprehend and leverage differences' (Shliakhovchuk, 2021: 236) and bring the *value* of cultural diversity into view. In the 21st-century skills framework, we continue to see this convergence of a citizenship project with the commodification of 'cultural' competencies. This can be understood critically as part of a wider instrumentalisation of education for producing marketable skills (Oinonen, 2018) or, more affirmatively, as a strategic duality that offers those with cultural expertise new opportunities in the 21st-century workplace (Ang, 2011).

There are few analyses of how race plays into the formation of these skills and competencies. The 'determinants' of 21st-century skills have been defined as personality, psychological and social factors (van Laar et al, 2020) but not with reference to a learner's racial or class positioning and how these structure their access to privileged kinds of knowledge. This problem might be attributed to an individualised understanding of 'skill' that has become part of labour market planning and which overlooks how designations of what counts as a 'skill' are political (Osterman et al, 2022). Despite its emphasis on cultural literacy, and efforts to address cultural complexity and volatility, '21st-century skills' risks becoming a universalising instrument. That is, it is a tool that supports diversity but obscures difference. In order for '21st-century skills' to be an economic and policy construct that can respond to inequality and racism, it must engage with the different capacities, experiences and embodied knowledge that different kinds of young people bring.

As the account in the next section shows, the creative industry workplace is structured by racial and ethnic inequality and exclusion. The skills discourse has the potential to either prepare young people to participate in these spaces or to contribute to processes that could transform them. To this end, it is worth asking whether 'cultural' competencies – which have their origins in global citizenship agendas to improve the world – could be imbued with a critical or transformative orientation. How, for example, might competencies such as cultural and civic awareness or (inter)cultural literacy relate to projects of anti-racism? We are interested in how the commodification of these competencies supports or undermines these critical agendas, and whether these critical orientations can be framed as part of the *value* of diversity in the 21st-century workplace.

Race and diversity at work in the creative industries

Young people globally face increasingly precarious labour markets. In many industrialised countries, higher education no longer guarantees secure employment, and a stable future is largely only available to those with access to intergenerational wealth (Oinonen, 2018; Cook, 2021). The kinds of precarity brought about by economic restructuring, and the role of younger generations in absorbing economic shocks (Brook et al, 2022: 37), are arguably worse for young people contending with racialised exclusion in the creative industries workplace. In Australia, despite 50 years of state multicultural policy, people of a non-European background are still grossly underrepresented in government, corporate and non-profit sector employment (Australian Human Rights Commission, 2018), as well as in arts and creative industry leadership (Diversity Arts Australia, 2019). Despite almost one quarter of Australians having a non-European or Indigenous background (Media Diversity Australia, 2022), and 29 per cent of Australians having been born overseas (Australian Bureau of Statistics [ABS], 2022), only 10 per cent of professional artists come from a non-English speaking background (Throsby and Petatskaya, 2017). Only 9 per cent of journalists come from a non-European background (ABS, 2022), and in 2022 more than 75 per cent of media presenters, commentators and reporters had a specifically Anglo-Celtic background (Groutsis et al, 2022).[1] These patterns of racialisation are obscured by the post-racial and post-multicultural vocabulary favoured by arts and cultural policy makers. Their turn to an 'aspirational diversity' (Khan, 2020) does not adequately acknowledge existing inequity in the creative industries and how race exacerbates young people's precarity in creative labour markets.

Much has been written about how the media and creative industries normalise precarity as the cost to be paid for a 'cool job' (Neff et al, 2005). In these industries, the risk of market failure and unpredictable business cycles is outsourced to individual workers as they wait for their next project or freelance opportunity (Cohen, 2012; McGuigan, 2014). Such conditions involve an interplay of autonomy and insecurity, variously described as 'flexploitation' (Morgan et al, 2013) or simply, 'a very complicated version of freedom' (Hesmondhalgh and Baker, 2010). It has been argued that young people's response to these conditions is the cultivation of entrepreneurial forms of subjecthood, where the willingness to take risks is part of a series of calculations aimed at increasing their value or 'cred' in the marketplace of human capital (Kelly, 2013; McRobbie, 2016). Here, entrepreneurialism is understood both as a mindset characterised by flexibility, self-reliance and resilience and as a set of practices aimed at continuous self-improvement (Brökling, 2016). Such individualised value adding involves an ethos of 'life-long learning' and the development of skills that are easily marketable (Oinonen, 2018: 1345). Micro-credentials have become a key instrument through which such skill development is given material recognition and market currency.

However, credibility is also accumulated more generally, via reflexive practices in which young people stitch together knowledge and competencies acquired from disparate life settings to narrate their value to the wider world. These efforts blur the boundaries between work and leisure and reflect the ways in which young people's subcultural and embodied capital have become central to their value as economic subjects. This is true of media and creative industry workers, as well as 'hipster' workers in the service economy, where one's value is shaped by disciplinary regimes of 'cool' and subcultural taste (McRobbie, 2002; Farrugia et al, 2018). Youth and creative industry scholars have shown how these regimes are formed and regulated through continual practices of boundary work, connected to gendered, classed and racialised hierarchies (Gill, 2002; McRobbie, 2002; Oakley and O'Connor, 2015). Such hierarchies structure the unequal distribution of subcultural capital and 'cred' and explain why, as the subsequent case study indicates, young people's pathways in the creative industries do not always correlate with their level of entrepreneurial effort.

Significantly for this analysis, formations of subcultural credibility shift over time. The gatekeeping of subcultural cred involves the continual stratification of consumption patterns and cultural practices, ascribing these different kinds of value in response to emerging trends. Subcultural cred reflects a scarcity principle, whereby it must stay ahead of its commodification at the same time that it is continually marketised. Studies of 'indie' subcultures ranging from music to extreme sports suggest how a brand's or artist's mass market success brings monetary rewards but can erode cachet (Dupont, 2014; Warren and Gibson, 2017). Creative enterprises aim to successfully leverage subcultural cred, but the mainstreaming of such cred also risks corporatisation and eventual delegitimisation. Such processes reflect the elusiveness of subcultural cred. While the advertising industry has long sought to define and capture 'cool' through market research and access to consumer data (Warren et al, 2019), this risk of co-option creates pressure for subcultural cred to keep evolving, by shifting and adapting its sources of legitimacy.

It is in this context that 'diversity' has become key to recent iterations of creative industry 'cred'. Despite the kinds of racialised exclusion that structure the arts and cultural sectors in Australia and other white-dominated and settler-colonial states, the global reverberations of anti-colonial and anti-racist movements such as Black Lives Matter have brought questions of race to the fore. These currents have motivated organisations, from fashion brands to state media broadcasters, to reflect on questions of diversity representation, implementing diversity quotas and more inclusive hiring practices (Groutsis et al, 2022). These efforts at inclusion, accompanied by more generalised affirmations of cultural and racial diversity, have become an important source of legitimacy for media companies wanting to signal good citizenship.

These recent developments converge with a longer-standing evaluation of diversity as both an expression of citizenship and as a resource for innovation (Khan, 2010; Bouncken et al, 2016). Studies of young Australian artists of migrant background have highlighted their practices of 'strategic essentialism', where diversity is knowingly deployed as an entrepreneurial tactic (Khan, 2013; Idriss, 2016). At the same time, diversity cred does not necessarily equate to egalitarianism or inclusive participation in the workplace. It has been argued that diverse workers still navigate settings that support diversity cautiously, attentive to 'how much ethnic identity one should demonstrate at different times to be a "safe bet"' (Edwards, 2013: 244). Such limits are tied to critiques of institutional 'diversity politics' which describe how difference is tolerated, commodified or consumed but not addressed through attention to wider structures of inequity (Ahmed, 2012). 'Diversity' can also operate in vague ways. As Rosalind Gill argues, support for diversity can be used to signify an 'unconventional, Bohemian, and informal atmosphere', referring to 'something other than identities tied to "race" or class or gender' (2014: 516). These kinds of slippages produce an ambivalent politics of credibility for diverse young people in creative industry workplaces. We now examine the marketisation of cultural diversity through the CMY Culture Spring programme.

Marketising culture: intersectional labour and the political economy of youth expertise in CMY's Culture Spring programme

To understand Culture Spring, it is critical to locate it in the longer trajectory, internal logic and institutional position of the CMY. The CMY was established in 1988 (originally as the Ethnic Youth Issues Network) in Victoria, Australia, as the first organisation in Australia to work exclusively with migrant and refugee young people. Its founding was motivated by a network of workers, many with lived experience of migration, who sought to 'break down barriers to services, create more opportunities for multicultural young people, and to name and tackle racism' (CMY, 2025). Over time, CMY has become an established, respected, specialist knowledge broker, bridging migrant/refugee youth, communities and the sectors (education, youth services, government) that aim to engage them (CMY, 2025).

CMY's vision is that young people from migrant and refugee backgrounds are 'connected, empowered and influential

Australians' (CMY, 2023). It delivers a suite of programmes that focus on educational support, community engagement, youth leadership, policy advocacy and capacity building for services to engage multicultural young people more effectively (CMY, 2023). For example, CMY's MY Education programme supports schools with resources, training and partnerships aimed at improving engagement with migrant/refugee students (CMY, 2023). CMY frames itself as an institution that 'shapes culture' not merely by service delivery but by shifting systems, structures, norms and power relationships. In celebrating its 35th anniversary, CMY describes '35 years of shaping culture' as integral to its identity (CMY, 2024).

As such, CMY emerges not simply as a service provider but as a mediating, translating and influencing organisation. It occupies an intermediate position between migrant/refugee young people and the institutions (government, schools, non-governmental organisations [NGOs], corporations) that purportedly seek to engage them.

Because CMY has institutional legitimacy, funding and standing, it is able to act as an 'expert' in multicultural youth engagement. However, as with many intermediary NGOs, it must navigate tensions: between serving as a critical actor that challenges inequities and fulfilling obligations to funders and institutional partners; between being accountable to community constituencies and to institutional clients.

CMY is situated in Victoria, but its claims and partnerships often have national significance: for instance, it has made submissions to federal policy reviews.[2] It thus acts as both a local anchor and a national voice for multicultural youth. Its role involves knowledge production – reports, frameworks, advocacy – as well as curated programming. In this context, Culture Spring can be understood as a strategic extension of CMY's institutional work: a youth-led social enterprise that attempts to manifest the principles of youth participation and cultural translation in a mode that can engage institutional and white audiences.

Culture Spring: structure, positioning and messaging

We now turn to Culture Spring itself, to see how it has been framed, marketed and organised, before engaging the theoretical critique. Culture Spring is presented as a youth-led social enterprise powered by CMY that 'bridges the gap between organisations and multicultural young people'. Its core proposition is that many organisations struggle to meaningfully engage multicultural young people and risk superficial, tokenistic or ineffective engagement. Culture Spring seeks to remedy that by offering 'culturally attuned strategies', youth engagement pathways and thought partnership to help organisations do better (CMY, 2026).

In the 'About' page, Culture Spring describes its vision as one 'where multicultural young people can drive, shape and become the change they want'. Its mission is 'to challenge and build new systems and structures so multicultural young people can thrive'. And its purpose is to 'bring the perspectives and experiences of multicultural young people to the forefront of your work … so that they are empowered to be active participants and leaders' (CMY, 2026). The governance of Culture Spring includes a management committee of young people with expertise, lived experience and passion.

In its public marketing, Culture Spring uses phrases such as 'expertise', 'culturally attuned strategies' and 'bridging' – signalling that it sees itself as delivering a specialised, intermediary service (CMY, 2026). Thus, the programme positions multicultural young people not merely as objects of service but as providers of knowledge, insight, translation and leadership to organisations that may lack those capacities.

Marketing, packaging and value proposition

Culture Spring is structured as a 'service offering' or consultancy. The language resonates with those in the corporate, governmental or NGO sectors: '[B]uild youth engagement and leadership pathways', 'innovative, culturally attuned strategies', 'help you build youth engagement in your business or community' (CMY, 2026).

They invite organisational clients to 'book a discovery call', a standard consulting or service sales technique. They also cultivate a visual identity (Instagram, LinkedIn) and brand presence as a youth-driven enterprise (CMY, 2026; Culture Spring, 2026). In that sense, Culture Spring is packaged as a kind of cultural consultancy, helping predominantly white or mainstream institutions to access (or leverage) the cultural expertise of multicultural young people. The marketing suggests that this expertise is a scarce, valuable resource, one that institutions must outsource if they wish to engage meaningfully in diversity, equity, inclusion and youth participation.

Thus Culture Spring effectively commodifies cultural and intersectional knowledge: it presents a system by which institutional actors can 'buy into' insight, co-design, facilitation and capacity building with multicultural youth voices. One can view this as an institutionalisation and professionalisation of what might otherwise be informal or grassroots cultural brokerage or youth leadership work. Because Culture Spring is youth led and governed by a committee of young people with lived experience, the programme garners some legitimacy and authenticity. This helps to buffer criticisms that institutional actors are merely 'using' multicultural voices. The youth leadership brand is part of the packaging: it asserts that the voices and practices are not tokenistic but grounded in real experience and expertise.

Further, because Culture Spring is a 'social enterprise', it embeds (or at least it claims to embed) social purpose into its operations: balancing profit or cost recovery with mission. This hybrid orientation helps situate Culture Spring in the interstitial space between charity and market. This institutional form is strategic: it allows Culture Spring to charge fees to or negotiate with institutional partners, thereby generating revenue and sustainability while tying back to CMY's mission of shifting institutional practices.

A Black feminist/intersectional lens: critiques and tensions

While Culture Spring presents many promising attributes, applying Black feminist and intersectional theory helps surface tensions and contradictions inherent in the marketisation of cultural expertise. One of the strongest critiques from Black feminist thought (hooks, 1989; Lorde, 2012; Collins, 2017) concerns the ways in which marginalised people are required to monetise their own pain, identity or cultural difference, often in conditions of structural inequity. In this context, Culture Spring asks multicultural young people – often people of colour, diaspora, intersectionally marginalised – to provide cultural insight, translation and facilitation, effectively selling cultural labour to institutions.

Black feminist scholarship warns that such arrangements can risk reducing rich, embodied, complex forms of knowledge into decontextualised 'cultural expertise' products, which in turn can be consumed by institutions in superficial, extractive ways. The labour of translation, emotional labour, bridging and representing marginalised voices is packaged, priced and sold.

In the capitalist marketplace, these forms of cultural labour often remain undervalued relative to more traditional forms of professional expertise (for example, science, technology, engineering and mathematics; legal; management). The demand to monetise such labour can impose burdens on young people who possess these forms of knowledge, especially when that labour is tied to identity and emotional investment.

Furthermore, Black feminist and intersectional critiques would ask: who exactly bears the burdens of this labour? Are young women of particular communities bearing disproportionate demands? Are emotional labour, relational labour and the burdens of representation being feminised and racialised? The marketed model may obscure these burdens under the veneer of 'youth leadership' and 'expertise'. Thus, the commodification of cultural expertise must be interrogated: how are the costs (emotional, relational, cognitive) distributed, and are they fairly compensated?

Intersectional theory emphasises the multiplicity of axes of identity (race, gender, class, sexuality, religion, migration status, disability). When institutions purchase 'cultural expertise' via Culture Spring, there is a danger that that expertise becomes flattened or essentialised: multicultural young people become 'culture brokers' or 'diversity experts' in a monolithic sense rather than recognised as intersectionally diverse individuals.

Culture Spring's marketing language, which speaks of 'bringing the perspectives and experiences of multicultural young people to the forefront', may inadvertently imply that there is a coherent, singular 'multicultural perspective' that can be accessed or mediated. That framing risks reducing complex intersectional difference into digestible categories that institutions can 'manage'.

From a Black feminist standpoint, this flattening is problematic because it overlooks how cultural experience is inflected by gender, migration history, generational difference, faith, sexuality, disability, socio-economic class and so on. Those intra-group differences may be elided in favour of a curated 'expertise package' that institutions can more easily consume.

An intersectional critique would push against the assumption that 'cultural competence' is a stable commodity rather than a constantly negotiated, contested practice. It would question whether institutional clients are prepared to engage in the messiness of difference, or whether they prefer sanitised, packaged cultural knowledge.

> The first time people heard Jalen spit, it was on a cracked phone speaker outside a youth centre in Perth. The beat was thin, the recording rough, but the words carried. Jalen was all rizz. He rapped about Country: not as metaphor, but as relation. About dust that held memory, fences that cut across songlines. About police cars that circled more often than buses. Someone filmed

it. Someone uploaded it. Within a week, it had travelled further than Jalen ever had.

By the time a scout from a major label reached out, the language around him had already begun to shift.

'Raw.'

'Authentic.'

'Important voice.'

The label flew him to Sydney.

The office overlooked the harbour. Glass walls, clean lines, a kind of curated openness. They spoke about vision, about platform, about amplifying voices that mattered. They referenced movements like Black Lives Matter, spoke about responsibility, about the need for the industry to change.

'We're committed to diversity', one executive said, leaning forward. 'Not just representation: real inclusion.' Jalen nodded, listening. He had learned early that listening was a form of reading the room.

The contract came quickly. There were clauses about image, about public appearances, about 'brand alignment'. There were also promises: studio time, promotion, collaborations. A pathway that felt, for a moment, like expansion rather than compromise.

His first single dropped three months later.

It was still about Country, but softened. The edges sanded down. Where his original lyrics named dispossession, the new version spoke in broader terms: 'roots', 'history', 'connection'. The beat was cleaner, heavier, designed for radio.

It charted.

Interviews followed. Photo shoots. Panels on diversity in the arts. He was introduced as a 'rising Indigenous voice', a phrase that hovered somewhere between recognition and category. At first, Jalen believed he could hold both.

In smaller venues, he performed older tracks: the ones that spoke directly about land rights, about the ongoing realities of colonisation in Australia. The crowd shifted when he did. Some leaned in. Others grew still.

After one show, his manager pulled him aside.

'That track', she said carefully, 'it's strong. But it's ... specific.'

Jalen waited.

'We just need to think about audience. About reach.'

The label began to position him more 'deliberately'. Campaigns highlighted his background, photos back on Country, carefully framed. Short documentaries about his 'journey'. He became, in their materials, a figure through which the company could signal its engagement with diversity.

Internally, they called it 'cred'. Not cynically. Not explicitly. But the logic was there: association with difference as a form of legitimacy. A way to demonstrate alignment with broader social currents without necessarily altering underlying structures.

Jalen felt it in the questions he was asked.

'What does your culture mean to you?'

'How does it feel to represent your community?'

Less often: 'What do you think about land rights?'

Almost never: 'What needs to change?'

He tested the boundaries.

During a live radio interview, he spoke about a recent dispute over land access. Named it directly. Connected it to ongoing patterns of exclusion.

There was a pause.

Afterwards, his publicist sent a message.

'Great energy today. Just a reminder to keep commentary aligned with campaign messaging.'

Aligned.

It was a soft word for a hard limit.

The second album was more successful than the first.

It leaned further into what the label called 'universal themes'. Identity, resilience, belonging: terms broad enough to travel, to be consumed without friction. His image circulated widely now. He was invited to speak at industry events about diversity, about inclusion, about the importance of representation.

On stage, beneath clean lighting and careful branding, he became part of a narrative the industry was telling about itself.

That it was changing.

That it was listening.

That it was, in some sense, accountable.

But outside those spaces, the conditions he had once rapped about remained. Communities still fought for recognition of land rights. Encounters with racism continued, structured not as isolated incidents but as patterns. The gap between what was represented and what was lived did not close.

Jalen felt that gap most sharply when he tried to write.

The words came, but they stalled.

Not because he had nothing to say, but because he understood, now, the calculus of saying it.

How much could be spoken without jeopardising the platform?

How much identity could be performed without becoming a 'risk'?

He found himself editing before writing. Translating his own thoughts into something more palatable, more calculable.

Safe.

One evening, back in Perth, he performed at a smaller venue under a different billing.

No major promotion. No label presence.

Halfway through the set, he paused.

'This next one', he said, 'isn't on the album.'

The beat dropped: simpler, closer to the one from that first recording. His voice shifted, too. Less measured. More direct.

He rapped about land again. About theft, not history. About systems, not stories. About the ways in which recognition could be offered without redistribution, visibility without change.

The room responded differently this time.

Not louder. But much more deeply.

After the show, a young artist approached him.

'How do you do it?' she asked. 'Get in there, I mean. Make it work.'

Jalen considered the question.

'It depends what you mean by work', he said.

What Jalen had come to understand: slowly, unevenly, was that diversity, in the industry he now inhabited, functioned as both value and limit.

It was valued as a sign of good citizenship, as evidence that organisations were responsive to global movements and local critiques. It was mobilised as a resource: something that could drive innovation, expand audiences, generate legitimacy.

But it was also managed.

Contained within parameters that ensured it remained legible, consumable, non-disruptive. Workers like Jalen learned to navigate those parameters, to calibrate their expression, to decide when and how to foreground aspects of identity.

Strategic, sometimes. Necessary, often.

But never neutral.

The label continued to promote him.

He continued to release music.

And somewhere between those two trajectories, a tension persisted.

Not a contradiction to be resolved, but a condition to be negotiated.

A space where diversity could be celebrated, circulated and sold, while the deeper questions it pointed to remained, more often than not, just out of frame.

Power asymmetries and the 'market capture' of justice work

Another critique from intersectional and critical feminist thought is the idea that justice or diversity work becomes absorbed and captured by market logics, resulting in co-option or dilution of more radical aims.

Culture Spring is, in part, aimed at white people engaging with non-white diaspora communities in Australia. That framing positions the (white) institutional actors as clients and multicultural youth as advisors. This can replicate traditional power asymmetries under a veneer of 'cultural inclusion' work. The shape of the relationship (client vs consultant) may unsettle more egalitarian, emancipatory aims.

From a Black feminist lens, marketing cultural knowledge to white institutions can risk reinforcing the very power structures one seeks to dismantle: white institutions externalise cultural labour rather than transforming their own internal systems, thus outsourcing responsibility. This may lead to superficial changes (training, panels, consultations) without deeper structural shifts in how institutions operate or distribute power. In other words, the marketisation of cultural knowledge might undercut accountability: it allows institutions to acquire 'diversity insight' as a service rather than being structurally compelled to share power or co-govern with multicultural communities. Moreover, market logics shape which voices are privileged: those who can package their knowledge as a market offering, who have institutional legitimacy and are adept at branding may gain advantage, potentially sidelining grassroots voices or less 'marketable' perspectives. This dynamic echoes critiques from intersectional feminists about the commodification of feminist or antiracist labour (for example, diversity training firms) and the tendency for institutional actors to pay lip service rather than embrace structural transformation.

Who 'owns' cultural knowledge, and how is value distributed?

A key question is: once cultural knowledge is extracted, translated, marketed and sold, who reaps value (financial, reputational, institutional)? Does Culture Spring ensure that income and recognition flow equitably to the young people whose lived experience constitutes much of the value? Or does much of the surplus accrue to organisational or institutional clients?

Black feminist critique would demand careful accounting of who owns intellectual and cultural property and whether the young people are remunerated fairly, recognised for their contribution and have control over how their stories are used. Without transparent mechanisms, there is a risk that the relationship becomes exploitative: multicultural youth provide insight, but the institutional clients and intermediaries benefit disproportionately.

Even in participatory or youth-led models, power over the design, pricing, narrative framing and the dissemination of knowledge may rest unevenly. Intersectional critique insists that these asymmetries be made explicit and contested, not hidden under professional branding. Moreover, the 'expertise' that is packaged is often tailored to white institutional sensibilities (palatable, incremental, risk averse). The most radical, disruptive critiques of institutional power may be filtered out or downplayed: they may be less commercially viable or less welcome to clients.

Culture Spring gives institutional actors access to what is termed 'expertise' in engaging multicultural youth. But from a Black feminist and intersectional standpoint, one must interrogate the politics of epistemic authority: who is authorised to speak as an 'expert' on multicultural engagement? Who certifies it? What are the criteria?

In traditional academia, credentialing and peer review mediate expertise. In cultural brokerage and diversity work, the validation often comes from institutional clients or funders. That dynamic can privilege voices that conform to institutional expectations.

Culture Spring's youth governance and lived-experience framing serve to grant epistemic legitimacy, but whether that legitimacy is accepted equally by institutional clients and community voices is not guaranteed. There is a risk that institutional clients will privilege those who 'speak their language', thereby sidelining more critical or dissenting cultural knowledges. Intersectional critique would urge reflexivity: how to avoid recreating new hierarchies of who speaks for 'culture' and who is silenced.

Despite the caveats, Black feminist theory and intersectionality also teach us to attend to agency, resistance and transformative potential. Culture Spring is not a monolithic site of co-optation; it also contains spaces of disruption, reorientation and boundary crossing. Because Culture Spring is youth driven, it offers young people an arena to exercise voice, leadership and curriculum control (at least to some degree). That can shift institutional relationships: rather than being passive recipients, young people become interlocutors and co-designers.

Also, through its interventions, Culture Spring may provoke deeper institutional introspection: not just 'how to engage multicultural youth' but 'how do we restructure ourselves to share power?' If cultural expertise is positioned not as a one-off service but as an ongoing relationship, institutions may begin to internalise cultural reflexivity and structural change. From a Black feminist-leaning praxis, the hope is that such initiatives can 'queer' institutional norms, inserting multiplicity, disruption and relational accountability into rigid bureaucracies. Thus, while culture-springing expertise is risky, it also contains the potential for destabilising hierarchical logics, if done with awareness, intentionality and accountability mechanisms.

Conclusion

This chapter has brought a critical race and Black feminist theory analysis to the discourse of 21st-century skills. It set out to ask what the discourse of 21st-century skills offers racialised young people, when 'culture' and 'diversity' have been historically positioned within this framework as both competencies for global citizenship and as commodities for globalised business. We have argued that while this skills discourse values (inter)cultural competencies, it is largely a universalising instrument that obscures cultural difference itself. It contributes to the instrumentalisation of cultural and racial diversity as the basis on which racialised young people can offer 'skills' for future economies. However, while the skills discourse promotes cultural literacy, as a workplace asset it cannot account for the unequal ways that cultural literacy is cultivated, inhabited and experienced by differently racialised bodies.

The problem of diversity is often understood as the problem of unequal access to the means of cultural production. However, the experiences of CMY's youth participants highlight that addressing the 'access' issue – perhaps through better recognition of learning and skills offered by a micro-credential framework – only offers a partial solution. While diverse young people in creative industry workplaces are learning skills of adaptation and resilience in the face of uncertainty, creative industry workplaces could themselves adapt to provide more secure and supportive spaces for diversity. A workplace that values 21st-century skills is not the same thing as a workplace that is inclusive. What the skills discourse might offer – through its emphasis on critical thinking, creativity and social and cultural literacies – is a way of supporting the kinds of critical leadership and intervention necessary to shift these dynamics of exclusion. A micro-cred framework potentially recognises the social and cultural knowledge that racialised young people offer, although it does not give explicit recognition of the critical, political dimension of this knowledge.

Young people cannot be awarded a micro-credential for being a person of colour in a white organisation – but at the same time it is on the basis of these embodied assets that young people are being valued, and excluded, in creative industry workplaces. Research that aims to develop tools for capturing young people's competencies could consider how to recognise the literacies acquired through embodied, lifelong practices of racialised self making.

SEVEN

Conclusion

Re-imagining and re-making the problem of young people and the future of work

This book has traced the long and shifting genealogy of how young people are framed as 'a problem' in public discourse, policy, education and the creative industries. From 19th-century anxieties about moral development and the need to discipline working-class children newly released from the factory floor, to 20th-century concerns with 'youth in trouble' and the post-war invention of 'problem youth' as a category of social research, through to contemporary policy discourses of skills, employability and entrepreneurship, young people have persistently been imagined as requiring intervention, correction or development. The problematisation of youth is not incidental but structural: it is the condition of possibility for entire domains of educational theory, youth policy and cultural programming. Young people are both 'in trouble' (facing poverty, marginalisation, climate precarity) and 'trouble' (figured as disruptive, risky, difficult to manage).

Our analysis has shown how these framings circulate across multiple fields of governance. In education, pedagogical technologies such as playgrounds, creative writing classes and arts programmes have historically been designed to cultivate ethical selfhood by eliciting expressions of individuality and creativity. In cultural policy, youth arts initiatives have functioned as mechanisms for managing unemployment, producing employability and legitimating creative industries agendas. In research, young people have been treated as experimental populations, figures through which to model futures, test policies or imagine social change. Throughout, the 'problem of youth' has been remarkably adaptable, shifting its form in response to new economic and social conditions while retaining its function as an object of governance.

Yet the persistence of this problem frame sits uneasily with the realities of contemporary youth life. Today's young people face conditions that exceed and destabilise older categories of governance. Economic precarity has deepened: the rising cost of education, the proliferation of casual and insecure work and the withdrawal of welfare supports mean that entire generations are unable to reproduce the life pathways of their parents. Structural inequalities of class, race, gender and disability remain entrenched and are often exacerbated by credentialist regimes that demand ever more qualifications for ever fewer secure jobs. Global crises – climate change, pandemics, political instability, the so-called sixth extinction – pose existential threats that dwarf traditional sociological concerns with delinquency, risk or deviance. Alongside these pressures, technological change, particularly automation and artificial intelligence, is transforming the nature of work in ways that remain unpredictable. The future of employment itself, once the bedrock of developmentalist assumptions about youth transitions, appears unstable.

Against this backdrop, the framing of young people as 'a problem' becomes increasingly inadequate, even misleading. It obscures the structural and planetary crises that shape youth lives while reproducing a narrow focus on behaviour, attitude and skill deficits. It locates responsibility in the individual young person – asking are they resilient enough, adaptable enough, employable enough? – while deflecting attention from the systemic failures of labour markets, education systems and political institutions. It continues to reproduce a deficit-oriented conception of youth, even as young people demonstrate remarkable creativity, resilience and capacity for collective action.

The ambition of this Conclusion is therefore not only to synthesise the arguments of the book but also to reframe the 'problem of youth' by foregrounding agency, creativity and the reconfiguration of work. Throughout the chapters, we have seen how young people are both subject to governance and agents of possibility. Programmes such as ATYP, The Push, Carclew, NGV Ambassadors and Future Foundations illustrate the ambivalent terrain where youth arts serve as both disciplinary apparatuses and spaces of experimentation. Historical examples such as Marcus Westbury's Octapod, or satirical cultural artefacts like *The Young Ones*, remind us of the unruly, excessive and 'wild' skills of youth that continually exceed institutional capture. By situating these practices within a critical account of governance, we can hold together two perspectives: the ways youth are governed through discourses of creativity, skills and employability, and the ways young people use creative practices to assert agency, forge identities and imagine futures beyond the limits of existing structures.

To reimagine the problem of youth is also to reimagine the future of work. If work is no longer a stable horizon of aspiration, if secure jobs, linear career pathways and the promise of social mobility through education can no longer be assumed, then new frameworks are needed for understanding how young people engage with work, skills and creativity. Micro-credentials, creative industries training and '21st-century skills' discourses are responses to this uncertainty, offering flexible pathways and modular recognitions of learning. But as we have shown, they also risk reproducing inequalities by shifting responsibility onto young people to endlessly upskill and adapt. Against this backdrop, youth creative practices can be understood not only as employability training but as forms of world building: ways of imagining and rehearsing futures that may not conform to existing labour market logics.

The stakes could not be higher. In precarious economies marked by automation and inequality, and in planetary conditions threatened by climate change and extinction, the problem is not simply how to integrate youth into work but how to reconfigure the very meaning of work, value and survival. This Conclusion argues that young people's creative agency, expressed through arts, media, cultural production and collective action, must be taken seriously as a resource for reimagining futures of work. By reframing the problem of youth not as a deficit but as a site of creativity, aspiration and skill, we can begin to see young people not only as objects of governance but as agents of transformation in times of crisis.

If the problem of young people is an enduring concern, it is because it has been so central to the organisation of education, culture and labour in modern societies. To speak of 'youth governance' is to point to the many institutional settings – schools, welfare agencies, creative industries, youth programmes – where young people are framed as requiring intervention, management or development. From the outset of public education systems in the 19th century, to the consolidation of youth studies in the 20th and into contemporary debates about skills and employability, youth have been positioned as both subjects in need of care and objects of regulation. The persistence of this problem frame is striking, not least because it adapts to shifting historical circumstances.

As Ian Hunter and other post-Foucauldian scholars have shown, the invention of public schooling was inseparable from questions of moral development. The playground, a seemingly benign technology of leisure, was in fact an apparatus for ethical surveillance: a space where children's 'true' characters could be observed outside the constraints of classroom discipline (Hunter, 1988). From here, creative and cultural education were annexed to the management of selfhood. Reading, writing and artistic expression became pedagogical techniques through which students were encouraged to reveal their interiority, while teachers were tasked with guiding that interiority towards desirable social and moral forms. The problem of youth was not delinquency per se but the opacity of selfhood: the fear that children's apparent obedience might conceal inner resistance or immorality. Creativity, in this sense, was never outside governance; it was one of its preferred tools.

By the mid 20th century, with the rise of youth cultures in consumer economies, the 'problem of youth' took on new dimensions. Young people with disposable incomes became the objects of marketing and media industries while also being subject to sociological scrutiny as risky, deviant or troublesome. The post-war emergence of 'problem youth' in research coincided with anxieties about rock and roll, juvenile delinquency and the disruptive energies of new cultural forms. Here too, creativity was double edged: it was both the marker of unruly subcultures and the channel through which youth could be re-integrated into society. Community arts and later youth arts programmes sought to mobilise creativity for social ends, offering spaces where young people could 'find their voice' while also being trained in the soft skills of teamwork, communication and resilience.

What is striking is how flexible the frame has been. As conditions shift, the problem of youth is re-articulated rather than abandoned. In the 1970s and 1980s, the decline of full employment and the rise of 'employability' as a policy goal produced new problematisations of youth unemployment. Youth were no longer framed only as risks to be contained but as untapped resources to be activated. Creative industries policy, as we have shown in earlier chapters, positioned youth as bearers of future skills: innovative, flexible, entrepreneurial, but only in so far as they could be disciplined into forms recognisable to policy agendas. The 'creative' young person was celebrated but in a highly circumscribed way: creativity was valuable when it was aligned with labour market needs, not when it manifested as punk excess or anarchic refusal.

Marcus Westbury's reflections on his youth arts work in Newcastle in the 1990s vividly illustrate this ambivalence. On the one hand, the establishment of Octapod and his later role in the LOUD festival demonstrate the agency of young people in creating their own cultural infrastructure in conditions of high unemployment. On the other hand, his experience as a 'professional token youth' underscores the instrumentalisation of youth presence in top-down cultural programmes. Westbury's account of being positioned as the public face of LOUD because he was young enough to match the target demographic captures the tension: youth are invited into governance structures but often in ways that reinforce their symbolic role rather than their actual agency (Westbury, 2006).

The satirical energy of *The Young Ones* in the early 1980s makes the same point in a different register. The parody segment 'Nozin' around', ostensibly a youth media program 'by young adults, for young adults', exposes the circular logic of policy discourses on unemployment. Youth media, far from offering solutions, becomes part of the problem by reproducing bureaucratic platitudes and deflecting attention from the structural causes of joblessness. That this satire occurred within a youth-targeted sitcom is telling: it reflects a moment of self-awareness within youth culture itself, recognising that even spaces of expression and creativity are caught up in cycles of governance and commodification. At the same time, the unruly humour, absurdity and sheer chaos of *The Young Ones* gesture towards something irreducible: a surplus of energy, creativity and critique that cannot be neatly folded back into policy frameworks.

This 'wildness' of youth skills – the unruly capacities, affects and improvisations that exceed institutional capture – is central to reimagining the problem frame. Post-governance critiques, as developed in this book, highlight how governance no longer operates simply through top-down discipline but through incitements to self-expression, creativity and participation. Young people are not only governed by being told what not to do; they are governed by being asked to express themselves, to be creative, to innovate, to aspire. As Anna Hickey-Moody and Scott McQuire have argued in their respective work, such post-governance techniques are seductive because they appear to affirm youth agency while actually steering it towards desired ends. Programmes that encourage youth creativity often come bundled with expectations of employability, resilience and self-management. The liberal apparatus of governance 'stays with the trouble' by incorporating the very resistances and wildness it seeks to manage.

And yet, even within this apparatus, the wildness of youth skills persists. Whether in the DIY ethos of punk bands, the collaborative experiments of youth collectives or the digital creativity of young people navigating new media ecologies, there is always an excess that cannot be fully instrumentalised. This is what makes youth governance both necessary and impossible: necessary because young people continually disrupt existing social forms, impossible because their energies cannot be entirely channelled into productive ends.

To recognise the persistence of the problem frame is therefore not to accept it as inevitable but to understand its historical durability and adaptive capacity. The governance of youth has always been a balancing act between containment and incitement, discipline and expression, problematisation and aspiration. Today, as we confront new crises of work, education and environment, the problem frame continues to shape policy and practice. But as this book has argued, it is precisely by attending to the ambivalences, contradictions and wildness of youth agency that we can begin to reimagine futures beyond the narrow horizons of governance.

In this light, the persistence of the problem frame can be seen less as a constraint than as a terrain of struggle. Youth are always already framed as problems, but they are also always already exceeding those frames, remaking themselves and their worlds in ways that elude capture. To reimagine youth agency is to hold onto this excess, to take seriously the creative practices through which young people navigate precarity and to recognise that the future of work will be shaped not only by policy and institutions but by the inventive capacities of youth themselves.

Skills, aspirations and the micro-cred economy

If the problem of youth has been historically tied to their unruliness, delinquency or lack of moral development, in contemporary discourse the problem is increasingly defined in terms of skills. The language of 'skills gaps', 'skills shortages' and 'skills for the 21st century' now saturates education policy, cultural industries initiatives and labour market strategies. Young people are less often described as morally suspect or socially deviant and more often framed as insufficiently skilled, under prepared or uncompetitive in global labour markets. The deficit remains, but it is recast: not a deficit of morality but of capacity. In this sense, the discourse of skills is the contemporary iteration of the 'problem youth' frame.

The notion of '21st-century skills' exemplifies this shift. Popularised by policy organisations, industry groups and educational think tanks, the term signals a cluster of competencies – creativity, collaboration, communication, critical thinking, adaptability, resilience – that are presented as essential for young people to thrive in the rapidly changing world of work. These skills are framed as universal, timeless and future proof, transcending specific industries or occupations. The implication is that while particular jobs may become obsolete through automation or globalisation, young people with the right portfolio of skills will always be employable.

Yet the discourse of 21st-century skills is riddled with contradictions. First, it assumes that the responsibility for managing economic uncertainty lies with the individual young person rather than with structural transformations of labour markets, welfare systems or industrial policy. To be 'future ready' is to constantly adapt, upskill and re-invent oneself.

The onus is on the individual to remain employable, rather than on employers or governments to provide stable work. In this sense, 21st-century skills are less a genuine recognition of youth creativity than a neoliberal responsibilisation strategy, shifting risk from institutions to individuals.

Second, the discourse is curiously vague. Terms like 'creativity' and 'resilience' are difficult to measure, standardise or certify. They operate as floating signifiers, open to multiple interpretations depending on context. This vagueness is not a weakness but a strength: it allows policy makers, educators and employers to invoke the discourse flexibly, to justify a wide range of programmes and interventions. As critics such as Bacchi (2009) remind us, what matters is not whether a problem representation is accurate but what it does: how it structures thought, channels funding and legitimises governance. The notion of '21st-century skills' does important work in rearticulating the problem of youth for contemporary times.

It is within this context that micro-credentials have emerged as a prominent response. Promoted by governments, universities and industry partners, micro-credentials are short, targeted qualifications that certify specific skills or competencies. Unlike traditional degrees, which require years of study and substantial financial investment, micro-credentials promise flexibility, affordability and responsiveness to labour market needs. They are often delivered online, assessed through digital platforms and stored as 'badges' or 'blocks' in digital wallets. The rhetoric is one of democratisation: anyone, anywhere, can gain recognition for their skills and remain competitive in volatile economies.

At first glance, micro-credentials appear to offer solutions to some of the problems identified in earlier chapters: the rising cost of education, the mismatch between qualifications and jobs, the barriers faced by marginalised groups. For young people who cannot afford a four-year degree, or who wish to gain quick recognition for skills developed informally, micro-credentials offer new pathways. For employers seeking agile workers, they provide reassurance of competence. For universities facing funding crises, they open new revenue streams. The appeal is broad and cross-sectoral.

But micro-credentials also raise critical questions. Whose skills are being recognised, and whose are overlooked? What forms of knowledge are made visible, and which remain invisible? While a micro-credential in coding or project management may be legible to employers, the skills cultivated through community arts, youth collectives or care work may not be so easily packaged. Moreover, the proliferation of micro-credentials risks intensifying credentialism itself: young people may find themselves in an endless cycle of upskilling, collecting badges to prove their employability without ever securing stable work. The promise of flexibility can quickly become the reality of precarity.

This tension is evident in the creative industries, where aspirations and skills are often entwined. As we have argued throughout the book, youth are encouraged to aspire to 'cool jobs' in music, fashion, media and the arts, jobs that are presented as both fulfilling and future oriented. Programmes such as The Push, Carclew and ATYP foster these aspirations, providing training in creative practice alongside employability skills. On one level, these programmes genuinely expand opportunities, supporting diverse young people to develop confidence, networks and capacities. On another level, they risk channelling youth creativity into narrow pathways aligned with industry needs, reproducing inequalities rather than overcoming them.

The concept of aspiration itself requires scrutiny. Aspirations are often framed as purely individual: what do you want to be when you grow up? But as scholars of social reproduction have shown, aspirations are deeply structured by class, race, gender and geography. Working-class young people may aspire to secure jobs and financial stability, while middle-class peers may aspire to self-realisation and creative fulfilment. The expansion of micro-credentialing risks amplifying these inequalities: those with cultural capital and financial resources can strategically accumulate credentials to enhance their CVs, while those without may end up with fragmented badges that fail to translate into meaningful opportunities.

The 'problem of youth' thus reappears in the micro-cred economy in new guises. Young people are told that the future of work is uncertain, but that with the right skills and credentials they can secure their place. The pressure to aspire, adapt and credentialise becomes itself a form of governance. The creative practices of youth, once valued as intrinsic expressions of identity, are reframed as potential evidence of employability. As Westbury reminds us, even the most grassroots cultural initiatives can be absorbed into policy agendas that instrumentalise creativity for economic ends.

And yet, to dismiss micro-credentials and 21st-century skills discourse entirely would be too simple. For many young people, these frameworks do provide opportunities otherwise unavailable. A badge earned through a youth arts programme may not be equivalent to a university degree, but it can still open doors, provide recognition and build confidence. The ambivalence is key: micro-credentials are both enabling and constraining, both empowering and disciplining. They can democratise access while also entrenching inequality.

The challenge, then, is to reimagine skills and credentials not merely as tools for employability but as forms of agency. When young people use creative practices to define their own skills, articulate their own aspirations and demand recognition on their own terms, they disrupt the deficit model that underpins skills discourse. Rather than being endlessly remade as 'not enough', youth can assert themselves as already skilled, already creative, already contributing to futures of work that exceed institutional categories.

In this sense, the micro-cred economy is a site of struggle. It reflects the ongoing problematisation of youth as lacking, but it also provides new spaces where young people can contest definitions of value and remake the meaning of skills. If creativity is persistently mobilised as a solution to the problem of youth, perhaps it is also the site where youth agency most forcefully asserts itself against being problematised. The next section explores how this ambivalence plays out in the creative industries, where partnerships, practices and possibilities both reproduce and reconfigure the problem of young people and the future of work.

The creative industries: between problem and possibility

The creative industries have become a privileged site where the 'problem of youth' is both reproduced and contested. Since the 1980s, cultural policy has increasingly positioned creativity as the solution to economic and social challenges: creative jobs are imagined as engines of growth, creative skills as antidotes to unemployment and creative programmes as means of engaging marginalised young people. For youth themselves, participation in arts and cultural projects promises empowerment, self-expression and pathways to employment. Yet as the case studies in this book have shown, this promise is ambivalent. The creative industries both absorb youth aspirations into neoliberal agendas and open spaces where alternative forms of agency and identity can emerge.

To understand this ambivalence, it is useful to recall the genealogy traced in earlier chapters. In the 1980s and 1990s, the shift from welfare to workfare coincided with the decline of manufacturing and the rise of cultural industries policies in countries such as the UK and Australia. Youth unemployment was reframed not as a structural outcome of deindustrialisation but as an individual deficit of skills and adaptability. Community arts and youth media initiatives were mobilised to address this deficit, offering training in communication, teamwork and resilience under the guise of creative expression. As Gay Hawkins (1991) observed, access to culture was never simply about empowerment; it was always tied to governmental agendas of reform.

At the same time, the creative industries offered real possibilities. For young people excluded from traditional education or employment, arts programmes provided spaces of belonging, recognition and experimentation. Youth workers and artists developed practices that valued diversity, creativity and collaboration. The field of youth arts was and remains administered to a great extent by young people themselves, producing a reflexivity and criticality not always present in other sectors. The very ambivalence of youth arts, caught between governance and agency, enabled it to serve as a laboratory for reimagining work, identity and community.

This ambivalence is evident in the contemporary programmes explored in this book: ATYP, Carclew, The Push, NGV Ambassadors and Future Foundations. Each illustrates how youth arts and creative industries initiatives simultaneously reproduce and challenge the problem of youth.

ATYP provides training and performance opportunities for young actors, writers and directors. Its workshops and productions cultivate skills that are highly valued in the 21st-century skills discourses, collaboration, communication and creativity, but they also do more. They enable young people to tell their own stories, to experiment with identity and to participate in collective cultural production. While ATYP is undoubtedly part of the creative industries pipeline, preparing some participants for professional careers, it is also a space where diverse young people can experience the intrinsic value of art. The tension lies in whether these intrinsic values can survive the instrumentalisation of creativity for employability agendas.

Carclew, a South Australian youth arts organisation, illustrates a similar tension. Its programmes support emerging artists across diverse practices, offering grants, residencies and workshops. Carclew's emphasis on diversity and inclusion aligns with policy priorities of equity and access, but it also reflects the lived realities of young people for whom creativity is not a luxury but a way of navigating identity and community. The skills developed through Carclew programmes, artistic, organisational, entrepreneurial, are readily aligned with creative industries discourse. Yet the organisation's work also demonstrates how youth arts can cultivate capacities that exceed market logics: resilience in the face of marginalisation, solidarity among peers and the capacity to imagine futures beyond precarity.

The Push, a youth music organisation based in Victoria, makes the ambivalence even clearer. Founded in the late 1980s, The Push has long been a training ground for young musicians, event organisers and cultural workers. On the one hand, it offers practical pathways into the music industry, teaching participants how to run gigs, manage events and build networks. These are precisely the employability skills celebrated in creative industries policy. On the other hand, The Push also fosters scenes, subcultures and peer-to-peer learning that are not reducible to employability. The skills acquired are not just 'job skills' but forms of cultural competence, identity work and creative experimentation. The Push exemplifies how youth music cultures are simultaneously harnessed by policy agendas and irreducible to them.

The NGV Ambassadors programme offers a further example. Designed to engage young people as cultural intermediaries, the programme positions participants as representatives of youth audiences, helping the gallery reach younger demographics. As with Westbury's experience in the LOUD festival, the role of 'youth ambassador' is ambivalent: it empowers young people to contribute but it also tokenises them as representatives of their demographic. The programme teaches valuable skills in communication, curation and cultural diplomacy, aligning with 21st-century skills discourse. Yet it also raises critical questions about whose voices are heard, how youth are positioned in institutions and whether representation equates to agency.

Future Foundations, a UK-based organisation, provides another angle, focusing on leadership, employability and personal development. Its programmes explicitly target the problem of youth by cultivating resilience, adaptability and entrepreneurialism. Here, the alignment with neoliberal skills discourse is clearest: participants are trained to be self-managing, self-improving and competitive. But even in this context, young people use the programme to build networks, develop confidence and articulate aspirations that may not align neatly with market logics. The very tools of governance can be repurposed for agency.

What these examples collectively demonstrate is the double life of youth arts and creative industries programmes. They are instruments of governance, addressing the problem of youth through skills training, credentialing and employability. But they are also spaces of possibility, where young people express creativity, forge identities and build communities that cannot be reduced to policy objectives. The ambivalence is not a flaw but a defining feature of the field.

This ambivalence also reflects broader dynamics in the creative industries. As Terry Flew (2012) has argued, the creative industries discourse positions culture as an economic driver, aligning artistic practices with innovation, entrepreneurship and growth. For young people, this alignment opens new opportunities but also new pressures: to be creative is to be employable, adaptable and productive. The value of creativity is measured by its economic return, not by its intrinsic worth or social meaning. Yet as the case studies show, young people continually reassert the non-economic values of creativity: self-expression, solidarity, joy, critique.

The challenge, then, is to hold both sides of the ambivalence in view. To dismiss youth arts as mere instruments of governance is to overlook the real agency, creativity and community they foster. To romanticise them as pure spaces of empowerment is to ignore their entanglement with neoliberal agendas. By attending to the double life of youth arts, we can better understand how the problem of youth is reproduced and reconfigured in the creative industries.

Ultimately, the creative industries exemplify the persistence of the problem frame and the possibilities of its reimagining.

Youth are invited into creative programmes as problems to be solved: lacking skills, needing pathways, requiring engagement, but they also use these programmes to assert agency, develop capacities and imagine futures beyond precarity. The problem and the possibility are inseparable. It is in this ambivalence that the future of work is being re-made.

Partnerships: tensions, negotiations and generative potentials

Partnerships have become a central mode of organising youth programmes and creative industries initiatives. Rarely do such projects emerge from a single institution or sector; more often, they are constituted through collaborations between government agencies, arts organisations, schools, community groups and industry stakeholders. The logic of partnership reflects broader shifts in governance, where responsibility for social outcomes is distributed across networks rather than held by the state alone. In youth arts and creative industries contexts, partnerships are presented as win-win arrangements: young people gain opportunities, organisations gain legitimacy and resources and governments demonstrate responsiveness to social concerns.

Yet partnerships are never neutral. They are sites of negotiation, tension and sometimes conflict. They bring together actors with divergent interests, priorities and power. They raise questions about who sets the agenda, whose voices are heard and whose goals are privileged. At the same time, partnerships can be generative, producing new forms of collaboration, new opportunities for young people and new possibilities for re-imagining work and creativity. To analyse partnerships is therefore to examine the political economy of youth programmes, as well as their affective and ethical dimensions.

In policy discourse, partnerships are framed as efficient, innovative and responsive. They allow governments to leverage resources from the private sector, community organisations and philanthropic bodies. They enable arts organisations to extend their reach and demonstrate social impact. They provide schools with access to expertise and programmes they could not deliver on their own. For young people, partnerships are supposed to translate into opportunities that would not otherwise exist: access to training, mentorship, resources and networks.

Behind this rhetoric lies a managerial logic of risk sharing and responsibilisation. Partnerships distribute responsibility for addressing the 'problem of youth' across multiple actors, making it harder to locate accountability. When a programme succeeds, all partners can claim credit; when it fails, blame can be deflected or diffused. This logic is consistent with broader trends in neoliberal governance, where the state retreats from direct provision while retaining oversight through performance metrics and funding conditions. Partnerships thus both extend opportunities and complicate accountability.

Tensions and negotiations

The partnerships examined in this book, such as those underpinning ATYP, Carclew, The Push, NGV Ambassadors and Future Foundations, reveal the tensions that partnerships inevitably entail. One recurring tension is between the instrumental and intrinsic values of art. Government agencies and corporate sponsors often support youth arts programmes because they promise measurable outcomes: reduced unemployment, improved employability, increased social cohesion. Arts organisations and youth participants, however, may value creativity for its intrinsic worth: self-expression, joy, identity formation. Negotiating these divergent values requires constant translation and compromise.

Another tension lies in power asymmetries. Not all partners come to the table with equal influence. Government agencies and funders often set parameters that smaller organisations must work within. Industry partners may impose commercial logics that do not align with community priorities. Schools may be constrained by curricular demands. In such contexts, the voices of young people themselves can be marginalised, even when programmes claim to be youth led or participatory. The NGV Ambassadors programme illustrates this ambivalence: while young people are given a platform within a major cultural institution, their role is shaped by institutional needs for audience diversification and branding.

Negotiations also occur at the level of practice. Delivering a youth programme requires aligning different organisational cultures, timelines and expectations. Arts organisations may prioritise creative experimentation, while schools demand curricular relevance. Funders may require quantitative evidence of impact, while youth workers emphasise qualitative outcomes. These negotiations can be frustrating, but they are also productive: they force organisations to articulate their values, adapt to constraints and find common ground.

Generative potentials

Despite these tensions, partnerships can be profoundly generative. By bringing together diverse actors, they create opportunities for cross-sectoral learning and innovation. A school–arts partnership may expose teachers to new pedagogical methods, while artists gain insight into educational structures. A collaboration between an arts organisation and an industry partner may generate resources that expand possibilities for young people, even if the partnership is shaped by commercial logics.

For young people, the generative potential of partnerships lies in the expanded networks and opportunities they provide. Participating in a programme like The Push not only develops musical or organisational skills but also connects young people to industry mentors, venues and audiences. Carclew's residencies and grants open pathways to professional artistic careers that would otherwise be inaccessible. Future

Foundations' leadership programmes link participants to networks of policy makers, entrepreneurs and international peers. These opportunities are not merely instrumental but can be transformative, shaping young people's identities, aspirations and sense of agency.

Partnerships also generate new forms of value. While funders may demand measurable outcomes in terms of jobs or qualifications, the lived experiences of participants often reveal more intangible benefits: confidence, solidarity, creative experimentation. These forms of value may not be easily captured in metrics, but they matter deeply to participants. Indeed, one of the critical potentials of partnerships is that they create spaces where such alternative forms of value can emerge and be recognised, even if only partially.

Partnerships as sites of contestation

To focus on the generative potentials of partnerships is not to romanticise them. Partnerships remain sites of contestation where broader struggles over youth, creativity and work are played out. They can reproduce inequalities, privileging well-resourced organisations and marginalising grassroots initiatives. They can instrumentalise youth creativity for corporate or governmental ends. They can entrench neoliberal logics of responsibilisation. But they can also be contested from within. Youth participants and arts workers often resist or subvert instrumental agendas, carving out spaces for alternative practices. A music event framed as employability training can also become a site of subcultural identity. A leadership programme designed to foster entrepreneurialism can also nurture solidarity and critique.

The ambivalence of partnerships mirrors the ambivalence of the creative industries more broadly. They are both mechanisms of governance and spaces of possibility. The key is to recognise their dual character rather than reducing them to either co-optation or empowerment. To study partnerships is to trace the negotiations through which values, resources and meanings are produced and contested. It is to acknowledge that governance always involves translation, compromise and resistance.

What would it mean to imagine a politics of partnership attuned to both tensions and potentials? First, it would require centring the voices of young people not just as beneficiaries but as partners in their own right. Genuine co-design, rather than tokenistic consultation, is essential. Second, it would require recognising and valuing the diverse forms of creativity, knowledge and agency that young people bring, rather than reducing them to measurable outcomes. Third, it would mean acknowledging power asymmetries within partnerships and working actively to mitigate them, ensuring that smaller organisations and marginalised groups are not sidelined.

At their best, partnerships can be more than managerial arrangements; they can be sites of collective world making. They can enable new alliances between institutions and communities, new forms of value that exceed market logics and new possibilities for youth agency. At their worst, they can reduce creativity to a tool of governance, instrumentalising young people's aspirations for policy agendas. The reality is usually somewhere in between, and it is in this in-between space, the site of tension, negotiation and potential, that the future of youth work and creativity will be forged.

Practices: skills, creativity and the work of doing

If partnerships constitute the organisational infrastructure of youth programmes, practices are their lifeblood. Partnerships provide frameworks, funding and legitimacy, but it is through the everyday practices of making, performing, collaborating and reflecting that young people experience creativity and develop skills. Practice is where the abstract promises of youth arts – employability, empowerment, resilience – are translated into lived activity. It is also where young people encounter the tensions and contradictions of governance most directly, as they are asked to embody both the expressive freedom of art and the disciplined adaptability of the employable subject.

Tammy's work emphasises that practice is not only about producing artworks or performances but about cultivating diverse skills that extend beyond artistic technique. Through creative practice, young people learn how to collaborate, negotiate conflict, manage projects, speak publicly and adapt to changing conditions. These are precisely the '21st-century skills' valorised in policy discourse, but they are also deeply embedded in the embodied, affective and relational dynamics of practice. They cannot be reduced to checklists or metrics; they are developed through doing, often in contexts of uncertainty and experimentation.

ATYP and the work of performance

ATYP provides a vivid example of how practice cultivates both artistic and transferable skills. In ATYP workshops and productions, young people learn to act, write and direct, but they also learn to listen, respond and collaborate. Rehearsals require punctuality, preparation and discipline, while performances demand confidence, adaptability and the ability to engage audiences. These practices mirror workplace competencies but are experienced in ways that are affectively charged and collectively meaningful. For many participants, the skills developed at ATYP are inseparable from the friendships, solidarities and identities forged through shared practice.

ATYP also highlights the double-edged nature of practice. On one level, theatre training aligns neatly with employability discourse: it teaches communication, teamwork and resilience. On another level, it opens space for young people to explore identity, voice and creativity beyond instrumental outcomes. The challenge for organisations like ATYP is to hold open this space of intrinsic value while navigating the pressures of funding regimes that demand measurable impacts. Practice, in this sense, is both the site where employability skills are cultivated and where youth resist being reduced to employable subjects.

The Push and the practice of music

The Push offers another perspective, grounded in music practice. Young participants learn how to organise gigs, manage events and perform in front of audiences. These activities cultivate practical skills in logistics, budgeting and technical production alongside artistic development. As with ATYP, the practices of The Push mirror workplace competencies, but they also sustain subcultures, scenes and identities that cannot be reduced to employability.

The Push illustrates how practice is always more than skill acquisition. Running a gig involves negotiating with venues, coordinating with peers and dealing with setbacks. Performing requires confidence, vulnerability and improvisation. These practices teach adaptability and resilience, but they also generate joy, solidarity and a sense of belonging. For many participants, the most valuable outcomes of The Push are not credentials or job prospects but the affective and cultural capacities cultivated through collective practice.

Carclew and the practice of diversity

Carclew foregrounds the diversity of practice itself. Its programmes encompass visual arts, performance, media and interdisciplinary projects, reflecting the multiplicity of young people's creative interests. Carclew's residencies and grants enable emerging artists to experiment with practice in ways that are not tightly bound to employability agendas. This openness is significant: it allows young people to pursue practices that may not translate directly into jobs but which are vital for identity, self-expression and cultural innovation.

At the same time, Carclew also trains young people in practical skills that support sustainable creative careers: project management, grant writing, budgeting and networking. These practices are less visible than performances or exhibitions but are crucial to navigating the precarious landscape of the creative industries. Carclew demonstrates that practice is not only about producing art but about learning how to sustain artistic work in real-world conditions. The combination of intrinsic and instrumental practices, artistic experimentation alongside practical management, reflects the ambivalence of youth arts in the creative industries.

NGV Ambassadors and the practice of representation

The NGV Ambassadors programme highlights another dimension of practice: representation. As youth ambassadors, participants practise speaking for and to their peers within a major cultural institution. They learn how to curate, communicate and engage diverse audiences. These practices cultivate skills in cultural diplomacy and institutional navigation, aligning with employability discourse. But they also raise critical questions about authenticity and tokenism: what does it mean to practise representation when one's role is defined by demographic identity?

For participants, the practice of being an ambassador can be both empowering and constraining. It provides access to networks, visibility and cultural capital, but it also positions young people as representatives of a group rather than as individuals. The practices of curation, consultation and communication are valuable, but they are shaped by institutional needs as much as by youth agency. NGV Ambassadors exemplifies the ambivalence of practice within partnerships: the skills learned are real and valuable, but they are cultivated in contexts where youth agency is both enabled and circumscribed.

Future Foundations and practice of leadership

Future Foundations explicitly frames its practices in terms of leadership and employability. Participants engage in workshops, projects and mentoring designed to cultivate resilience, adaptability and entrepreneurial thinking. The practices here are tightly aligned with neoliberal skills discourse: young people are trained to be self-managing, self-improving and competitive. Yet even in this context, the lived experience of practice exceeds the instrumental framework. Participants build friendships, gain confidence and develop solidarities that may challenge rather than reinforce neoliberal individualism.

The practice of leadership is therefore ambivalent. On one hand, it reproduces the responsibilisation of youth, training them to adapt to precarious economies. On the other hand, it provides young people with tools that can be repurposed for collective action, critique or alternative futures. The generative potential of practice lies precisely in this excess: the capacities developed cannot be fully contained within policy agendas.

The importance of practice

Taken together, these examples underscore the importance of practice in re-imagining the problem of youth and the future of work. Practice is where skills are embodied, where identities are forged and where agency is exercised. It is also where the ambivalences of governance are most palpable: young people practise creativity in ways that are both enabled by and resistant to policy frameworks.

Practice is not simply the application of abstract skills but a mode of being in the world. It involves improvisation, adaptation and negotiation. It is relational, affective and embodied. These dimensions are often overlooked in policy discourse, which treats skills as discrete, measurable and transferable. By attending to practice, we see how skills are lived, how they are embedded in cultural and social contexts and how they are inseparable from questions of identity and agency.

In this light, the 'problem of youth' cannot be reduced to deficits of skill or aspiration. What matters is how young people practise creativity, how they negotiate tensions and how they use practice to navigate precarious futures. Whether in theatre, music, visual arts or leadership programmes, practice is where young people remake themselves and their worlds. It is through practice that the future of work is being reimagined: not as a fixed horizon of jobs and credentials but as a fluid terrain of creativity, collaboration and possibility.

Possibilities: cool jobs for diverse young people

If partnerships provide the institutional scaffolding and practices embody the lived labour of youth creativity, then possibilities mark the horizon towards which these energies are directed. Possibility is what sustains youth aspirations, what justifies investment in youth programmes and what animates policy discourses about skills and futures. It is also what young people themselves generate through their creativity, resilience and refusal to be contained by the narrow logics of governance. Possibilities, however, are not neutral: they are unequally distributed, structured by inequalities of class, race, gender, disability and geography. To speak of 'cool jobs for diverse young people' is to acknowledge both the allure of aspirational futures and the challenges of making those futures real.

The allure of cool jobs

Cultural industries policy and youth arts programmes often hold out the promise of 'cool jobs' as a way of engaging young people. Work in music, film, design, fashion, gaming or digital media is presented as exciting, creative and future oriented. These jobs are imagined as antidotes to the drudgery of traditional labour, offering self-expression, flexibility and fulfilment. For governments, they are attractive because they signal alignment with innovation and growth agendas. For arts organisations, they provide a way of demonstrating relevance and impact. For young people, they represent aspirational pathways that resonate with their cultural interests and identities.

The problem, as we have seen, is that the promise of cool jobs often exceeds the reality. The creative industries are notoriously precarious, marked by short-term contracts, freelance work and competition for limited opportunities. Success stories exist, but they are often the exception rather than the norm. Many young people who pursue creative careers find themselves cycling between underpaid gigs, unpaid internships and unrelated jobs to make ends meet. The allure of cool jobs can therefore mask structural inequalities, presenting precarious work as desirable and individualising the risks of failure.

Diverse young people and unequal possibilities

The challenges are amplified for diverse young people: those from low-income backgrounds, Indigenous communities, migrant families or with disabilities. Structural barriers such as financial insecurity, lack of networks and discrimination limit access to creative opportunities. Programmes like ATYP, Carclew, The Push and NGV Ambassadors play an important role in addressing these barriers by providing resources, mentoring and supportive communities. They create possibilities that might otherwise be inaccessible. But even here, inequalities persist. Those with cultural capital and financial support are often better positioned to take advantage of opportunities, while others may struggle to translate participation into sustainable careers.

Possibility, then, must be understood not only as an abstract horizon but as a field structured by power. Who gets access to cool jobs? Who is recognised as talented, employable or creative? Whose cultural expressions are valued, and whose are marginalised? These questions remind us that the problem of youth is not only about deficits but about unequal distributions of possibility.

Youth programmes as engines of possibility

Despite these challenges, youth programmes generate real possibilities for young people. ATYP nurtures emerging playwrights, actors and directors, some of whom go on to professional careers in theatre and film. The Push supports young musicians to develop not only artistic skills but also industry knowledge, leading to opportunities in event management, production and the music industry. Carclew's grants and residencies provide crucial support for young artists to experiment and sustain creative practice. NGV Ambassadors offers pathways into cultural institutions, fostering curatorial and communication skills. Future Foundations cultivates leadership capacities that can translate into diverse career trajectories.

These programmes show that possibility is not only about the end point – securing a job – but about the process of cultivating confidence, networks and identities. For many participants, the most valuable outcome is not a specific job but a sense of expanded horizons: the belief that new futures are imaginable and attainable. In this sense, youth programmes are engines of possibility, generating affective and cognitive capacities that extend beyond measurable outcomes.

The double life of possibility

As with partnerships and practices, the discourse of possibility has a double life. On one hand, it aligns with neoliberal agendas that promote aspirational individualism: if you dream big and work hard, you can succeed. This narrative can obscure structural inequalities, placing responsibility on young people to create their own opportunities. On the other hand, the lived experiences of youth programmes show that possibility is also collective, relational and resistant. Young people create possibilities for one another through collaboration, solidarity and shared practice. They carve out spaces where different futures can be imagined, even in the face of precarity.

The double life of possibility is evident in Westbury's reflections on Octapod and LOUD. These projects emerged in contexts of economic crisis, where youth unemployment was rampant. They created real opportunities for young people to develop skills, gain visibility and build careers. But they also revealed the tensions of being positioned as 'token youth', instrumentalised for institutional agendas. Possibility here was both constrained and enabled: shaped by governance but also exceeding it.

Possibility as world making

To think about possibility in relation to youth creativity is to think about world making. When young people write plays, organise gigs, curate exhibitions or lead projects, they are not only preparing for future jobs; they are actively remaking cultural and social worlds. They are asserting identities, building communities and experimenting with forms of value that cannot be reduced to economic returns. Possibility is not just about entering the labour market but about reimagining what work, creativity and community might mean.

This world-making dimension is especially significant in the context of global crises. As climate change, automation and political instability disrupt existing structures, the futures available to young people are uncertain. Possibility, in this context, is not guaranteed by policy or industry but must be created through collective imagination and practice. Youth arts and creative industries programmes become laboratories for such imagination, spaces where alternative futures are rehearsed and made tangible.

Towards equitable possibilities

The challenge is to ensure that the possibilities generated by youth programmes are not limited to the privileged few but are equitably distributed. This requires attention to structural barriers: the rising cost of education, the precarity of creative industries and the inequalities of class, race, gender and disability. It also requires recognising the diverse forms of value that young people create, beyond employability metrics. Possibility must be understood not only as access to jobs but as the capacity to live meaningful, creative and sustainable lives.

Equitable possibility also demands rethinking the role of institutions. Rather than using youth programmes primarily as tools to produce employable workers, institutions could support them as sites of cultural innovation, community building and social critique. This would mean valuing the intrinsic worth of creativity alongside its instrumental outcomes and recognising young people as partners in shaping futures, not just as problems to be solved.

Conclusions and generative futures

In the creative industries, the promise of cool jobs functions both as a lure and as a trap. It engages young people by aligning with their aspirations, but it also risks masking precarity and inequality. Yet within this ambivalence lie real generative potentials. Youth programmes create spaces where possibilities are not just imagined but enacted, where young people practise world making in ways that exceed governance.

To speak of 'cool jobs for diverse young people' is therefore to hold onto this ambivalence. Cool jobs are not panaceas, but neither are they illusions. They are part of a larger ecology of possibility in which young people navigate structural constraints, institutional agendas and their own creative desires. By foregrounding the double life of possibility – its alignment with governance and its capacity for resistance – we can better understand how young people are reimagining the problem of youth and remaking the future of work.

Notes

one Introduction

[1] TAFE stands for Technical and Further Education.

[2] Digital Audio Workstations.

three The futures of skills, work and credentialing

[1] This discussion draws on Kelly (2013).

[2] This section draws on some of the arguments developed in Carbajo and Kelly (2019, 2023) and Goring et al (2023).

[3] See Chapter Five for further discussion of the complexities of developing 'creative' skills through a discussion of Bloom's 'Taxonomy of educational objectives' (Bloom et al, 1956), and Chapter Six for a race critical analysis of the discourse of 21st-century skills.

five Practices

[1] In recent years, the terms 'majority world' and 'minority world' have been adopted to replace 'developing' and 'developed' world (as referred to in the WEF's report) to create more equal and less hierarchical representation of categories of countries (see, for example: Lawrence, 2022).

six Diverse economies

[1] Of the total sample, 6 per cent had an Indigenous or non-European background (Groutsis et al, 2022).

[2] See https://www.cmy.net.au/organisations-businesses/policy-research/

References

ACER (2013) 'Using data to enhance 21st-century skill development in VET: discussion paper for the Summit on Data for Quality Improvement in VET', ACER.

Adams, C.N. (2019) 'Schools: Theatre of the Oppressed with youth', in K. Howe, J. Boal and J. Soeiro (eds) *The Routledge Companion to Theatre of the Oppressed*, Routledge, pp 322–9.

Ahmed, S. (2012) *On Being Included: Racism and Diversity in Institutional Life*, Duke University Press.

Alper, M. (2019) 'Future talk: accounting for the technological and other future discourses in daily life', *International Journal of Communication*, 13: 715–35.

Anderson, L.W. and Krathwohl, D.R. (2001) *A Taxonomy for Learning, Teaching, and Assessing: A Revision of Bloom's Taxonomy of Educational Objectives*, Longman.

Ang, I. (2001) *On Not Speaking Chinese: Living between Asia and the West*, Routledge.

Ang, I. (2011) 'Navigating complexity: from cultural critique to cultural intelligence', *Continuum*, 25(6): 779–94.

Appadurai, A. (1988) *The Social Life of Things: Commodities in Cultural Perspective*, Cambridge University Press.

Armstrong, P. (2005) *Critique of Entrepreneurship: People and Policy*, Palgrave Macmillan.

Armstrong, P. (2010) 'Bloom's taxonomy', Vanderbilt University Centre for Teaching, [online], Available from: https://web.archive.org/web/20240509033428/https://cft.vanderbilt.edu/guides-sub-pages/blooms-taxonomy/

ABS (2022) 'Australia's population by country of birth', ABS, [online], Available from: https://www.abs.gov.au/statistics/people/population/australias-population-country-birth/latest-release

ARC (2025) 'Linkage projects', [online], Available from: https://www.arc.gov.au/funding-research/funding-schemes/linkage-program/linkage-projects

ATYP (2022) 'A Clockwork Orange, Australian Theatre for Young People', [online], Available from: https://web.archive.org/web/20250328112535/https://atyp.com.au/ATYP-productions/a-clockwork-orange/

Australian Government (2022) 'Links to 21st-century learning', Australian Government, Department of Education, [online], Available from: https://www.education.gov.au/australian-curriculum/national-stem-education-resources-toolkit/i-want-know-about-stem-education/what-works-best-when-teaching-stem/links-21st-century-learning

Australian Human Rights Commission (2018) 'Leading for change: a blueprint for cultural diversity and inclusive leadership revisited', Australian Human Rights Commission.

Bacchi, C. (2009) *Analysing Policy*, Pearson Higher Education AU.

Bauman, Z. (2001) *The Individualized Society*, Polity.

Bauman, Z. (2004) *Wasted Lives: Modernity and Its Outcasts*, Polity.

Bauman, Z. (2005) *Work, Consumerism and the New Poor*, Open University Press.

Bauman, Z. (2007) *Consuming Life*, Polity.

Bazzani, G. (2023) 'Futures in action: expectations, imaginaries and narratives of the future', *Sociology*, 57(2): 382–97.

Beck, U. (2000) *The Brave New World of Work*, Polity.

Bennett, T. (1998) 'Cultural studies: a reluctant discipline', *Cultural Studies*, 12(4): 528–45.

Berown, P., Souto-Otero, M. and Sadik, S. (2022) 'Digital transformation and the future of work', *Digital Society*, 559.

Biesta, G.J. (2011) *Learning Democracy in School and Society*, Sense Publishers.

Blackmore, J. (1992) 'The gendering of skill and vocationalism in twentieth-century Australian education', *Journal of Education Policy*, 7(4): 351–77.

Bloom, B.S., Engelhart, M.D., Furst, E.J., Hill, W.H. and Krathwohl, D.R. (1956) *Taxonomy of Educational Objectives: The Classification of Educational Goals*, David McKay Company.

Borup, M., Brown, N., Konrad, K. and van Lente, H. (2006) 'The sociology of expectations in science and technology', *Technology Analysis & Strategic Management*, 18(3–4): 285–98.

Boukhari, S. (2025) 'Intersections of peace: refugee children's unique perspectives through storytelling and arts-based methods', *Journal of International Migration and Integration*, 26(2): 1037–63.

Bouncken, R.B., Brem, A. and Kraus, S. (2016) 'Multi-cultural teams as sources for creativity and innovation: the role of cultural diversity on team performance', *International Journal of Innovation Management*, 20(1): 1650012.

Bourdieu, P. (1993 [1978]) 'Youth is just a word', in P. Bourdieu, *Sociology in Question*, SAGE, pp 94–102.

Bourdieu, P. (1986) 'The forms of capital', in J. Richardson (ed) *Handbook of Theory and Research for the Sociology of Education*, Greenwood, pp 241–58.

Braudel, F. (1987) *Grammaire des civilisations*, Arthaud.

Bröckling, U. (2016) *The Entrepreneurial Self: Fabricating a New Type of Subject*, SAGE.

Brook, S. (2012) 'Creative writing, cultural capital and the labour market', *Australian Humanities Review*, 53: 1–10.

Brook, S. (2015) 'The exemplary economy: a Hunterian reading of the creative industries as educative project', *International Journal of Cultural Policy*, 22(1): 27–40.

Brook, S., Lee, J.Y. and Sun, M. (2022) 'Creative graduates and the labour market', in S. Brook, R. Comunian, J. Corcoran, A. Faggian, S. Jewell and J. Webb (eds) *Gender and the Creative Labour Market*, Palgrave, pp 29–52.

Budge, K. (2016) 'Teaching art and design: communicating creative practice through embodied and tacit knowledge', *Arts and Humanities in Higher Education*, 15 (3–4): 432–45.

Bulfin, S. and North, S. (2007) 'Negotiating digital literacy practices across school and home: case studies of young people in Australia', *Language and Education*, 21(3): 247–63.

Burgess, J., Foth, M. and Klaebe, H. (2006) 'Everyday creativity as civic engagement: a cultural citizenship view of new media', in F. Papandrea (ed) *Proceedings 2006 Communications Policy & Research Forum*, Network Insight Institute, pp 1–16.

Bermúdez, J. (2023) 'Performing beyond the platform: experiencing musicking on and through YouTube, TikTok, and Instagram', in H. Rogers, J. Freitas and J.F. Porfírio (eds) *Remediating Sound: Repeatable Culture, YouTube and Music*, Bloomsbury Academic, pp 187–202.

Campbell, M. (2019) 'From youth engagement to creative industries incubators: models of working with youth in community arts settings', *Review of Education, Pedagogy, and Cultural Studies*, 41(3): 164–92.

Carbajo, D. and Kelly, P. (2019) 'Young people, precarity and global grammars of enterprise: some preliminary provocations', *Recerca*, special issue: New forms of precariousness in the digital work era, 24(1): 61–91.

Carbajo, D. and Kelly, P. (2023) 'COVID-19, young people and the futures of work: re-thinking global grammars of enterprise', *The Sociological Review*, 71(1): 65–84.

Catterall, J.S. (2009) *Doing Well and Doing Good by Doing Art: The Effects of Education in the Visual and Performing Arts on Achievements and Values of Young Adults*, Imagination Group.

Catterall, J.S., Dumais, S.A. and Hampden-Thompson, G. (2012) 'The arts and achievement in at risk youth: findings from four longitudinal studies', National Endowment for the Arts, Available from: https://files.eric.ed.gov/fulltext/ED530822.pdf

Cieslik, M. and Simpson, D. (2017) 'The influences of basic skills and literacy practices on youth transitions and identities', in A. Furling (ed) *Routledge Handbook of Youth and Young Adulthood* (2nd edn), Routledge, pp 99–106.

Clammer, J. (2023) 'The creative self: artistic performance and the making and finding of identity', in M. Bussey, M. Chakravorty and C. Mozzini-Alister (eds) *Transitional Selves: Possibilities for Identity in a Plurified World*, Routledge, pp 33–48.

CLOCK Your Skills (2025) 'CLOCK Your Skills', Available from: https://clockyourskills.com/

CMY (2023) 'CMY submission to the inquiry into state education system: October 2023', Available from: https://www.parliament.vic.gov.au/495ec3/contentassets/a3718685f3e94a05853f21c8877e668b/196.-centre-for-multicultural-youth.pdf

CMY (2024) '35 years of shaping culture', Available from: https://www.cmy.net.au/cmy-news/35-years-of-shaping-culture/

CMY (2025) 'About us', Available from: https://www.cmy.net.au/about-us/

CMY (2026) 'About Culture Spring', Available from: https://www.cmy.net.au/culturespring-about/

Coffey, J. and Farrugia, D. (2013) 'Unpacking the black box: the problem of agency in the sociology of youth', *Journal of Youth Studies*, 17(4): 461–74.

Cohen, N. (2012) 'Cultural work as a site of struggle: freelancers and exploitation', *tripleC*, 10(2): 141–55.

Collins, P.H. (2017) 'Intersectionality and epistemic injustice', in I.J. Kidd, J. Medina and G. Pohlhaus (eds) *The Routledge Handbook of Epistemic Injustice*, Routledge, pp 115–24.

Cook, J. (2021) 'Keeping it in the family: understanding the negotiation of intergenerational transfers for entry into homeownership', *Housing Studies*, 36(8): 1193–1211.

Cook, J., Threadgold, S., Farrugia, D. and Coffey, J. (2021) 'Youth, precarious work and the pandemic', *Young* [online first]: 1–18, Available from: https://journals.sagepub.com/doi/full/10.1177/11033088211018964

Cremin, L.A. (1964) *The Transformation of the School: Progressivism in American Education, 1876–1957*, Vintage Books.

Csikszentmihalyi, M. (1991) *Flow: The Psychology of Optimal Experience*, Harper Perennial.

Culture Spring (2026) 'Culture Spring' [LinkedIn], Available from: https://au.linkedin.com/company/culturespring

Darling, N. (2007) 'Ecological systems theory: the person in the center of the circles', *Research in Human Development*, 4(3–4): 203–17.

De Roeper, J. and Savelsberg, H.J. (2009) 'Challenging the youth policy imperative: engaging young people through the arts', *Journal of Youth Studies*, 12(2): 209–25.

Deleuze, G. and Guattari, F. (2007) *A Thousand Plateaus*, University of Minnesota Press.

Derrida, J. (1976) *Of Grammatology*, Johns Hopkins University Press.

Department of Education (2024) 'Australian universities accord: final report', Available from: https://www.education.gov.au/australian-universities-accord/resources/final-report

Dewey, J. (1956 [1899]) *The Child and the Curriculum: And the School and Society*, University of Chicago Press.

Diversity Arts Australia (2019) 'Shifting the balance: cultural diversity in leadership within the Australian arts, screen and creative sectors', BYP group and Western Sydney University.

Dupont, T. (2014) 'From core to consumer: the informal hierarchy of the skateboard scene', *Journal of Contemporary Ethnography*, 43(5): 556–81.

Duxbury L., Grierson E.M. and Waite, D. (2008) *Thinking through Practice: Art as Research in the Academy*, RMIT Publishing.

Earley, P.C. and Ang, S. (2003) *Cultural Intelligence: Individual Interactions across Cultures*, Stanford University Press.

EC (2012) 'Entrepreneurship 2020 action plan: reigniting the entrepreneurial spirit in Europe', European Union, Available from: https://eur-lex.europa.eu/LexUriServ/LexUriServ.do?uri=COM:2012:0795:FIN:en:PDF

Edwards, L. (2013) 'Institutional racism in cultural production: the case of public relations', *Popular Communication*, 11: 242–56.

Ehrenreich, B. (2002) *Nickel and Dimed: Undercover in Low-Wage USA*, Granta Books.

Eldredge, N. (2001) 'The sixth extinction', American Institute of Biological Sciences.

EYF (2020a) 'The European youth blueprint to recovery', EYF, Available from: https://www.youthforum.org/files/blueprint.pdf

EYF (2020b) 'Youth & COVID-19: impacts on jobs, education, rights and mental wellbeing', EYF, Available from: https://www.youthforum.org/files/Youth-and-COVID-19-Survey-Report_English.pdf

Farrugia, D. (2019) 'Class and the post-Fordist work ethic: subjects of passion and subjects of achievement in the work society', *The Sociological Review*, 67(5): 1086–1101.

Farrugia, D. (2020) 'Youth, work and "career" as a way of talking about the self', *Work, Employment and Society* [online first]: 1–16, Available from: https://journals.sagepub.com/doi/full/10.1177/0950017020947576

Farrugia, D., Threadgold, S. and Coffey, J. (2018) 'Young subjectivities and affective labour in the service economy', *Journal of Youth Studies*, 21(3): 272–87.

Fehér, K., Junaidy, D.W., Larasati, D., Kovács, Á. and Rahardio, B. (2017) 'Prospects of creative industries and digital economy: perspectives from Southeast Asia and Central Europe', in T. Novak (ed) *Go Hungary – Go Indonesia: Understanding Economic and Business Issues*, Budapest Business School, University of Applied Sciences, pp 151–72.

Fergusson, R. and Yeates, N. (2021) *Global Youth Unemployment: History, Governance and Policy*, Edgar Elgar Publishing.

Flew, T. (2012) *The Creative Industries: Culture and Policy*, SAGE.

Foucault, M. (1980) *Power/Knowledge: Selected Interviews and Other Writings, 1972–1977*, Doubleday.

Foucault, M. (2008) *The Birth of Biopolitics: Lectures at the Collége de France, 1978–79*, Palgrave Macmillan.

Frow, J. (1995) *Cultural Studies and Cultural Value*, Clarendon Press.

Furlong, A. and Kelly, P. (2005) 'The Brazilianisation of youth transitions in Australia and the UK?', *Australian Journal of Social Issues*, 40(2): 207–25.

FYA (2015) 'The new work order: ensuring young Australians have skills and experience for the jobs of the future, not the past', FYA.

FYA (2017) 'The new basics: big data reveals the skills young people need for the new work order', FYA.

Gill, R. (2002) 'Cool, creative and egalitarian?', *Information, Communication & Society*, 5(3): 70–89.

Gill, R. (2014) 'Unspeakable inequalities: post-feminism, entrepreneurial subjectivity, and the repudiation of sexism among cultural workers', *Social Politics*, 21(4): 509–28.

Goldman, S., Booker, A. and McDermott, M. (2008) 'Mixing the digital, social, and cultural: learning, identity, and agency in youth participation', in D. Buckingham (ed) *Youth, Identity, and Digital Media*, MIT Press, pp 185–216.

Goring, J. (2023) 'Young people, 21st-century skills and uncertain futures: a genealogy of Australia's neo-liberal education apparatus', unpublished PhD thesis, Deakin University.

Goring, J., Kelly, P., Carbajo, D. and Brown, S. (2023) 'Young people's presents and futures, and the moral obligation to be enterprising and aspirational in times of crisis', *Futures*, 147: 103099.

Groutsis, D., Martin, L., Lattouf, A., Soutphomamasane, T., Lumby, C., Young, N. et al (2022) 'Who gets to tell Australian stories? 2.0', University of Sydney and Media Diversity Australia.

Gunnestad, A. (2006) 'Resilience in a cross-cultural perspective: how resilience is generated in different cultures', *Journal of Intercultural Communication*, 6(1): 1–21.

Halberstam, J. (2020) *Wild Things: The Disorder of Desire*, Duke University Press.

Hage, G. (1998) *White Nation: Fantasies of White Supremacy in a Multicultural Society*, Pluto Press.

Hahn, T.N. (2014) *Peace of Mind*, Transworld Publishers.

Hall, S. and Jefferson, T. (2006) *Resistance through Rituals: Youth Subcultures in Post-war Britain*, Routledge.

Hardt, M. and Negri, A. (2004) *Multitude*, Penguin.

Harris, A. (2017) 'Young people, politics and citizenship', in A. Furlong (ed) *Routledge Handbook of Youth and Young Adulthood* (2nd edn), Routledge, pp 295–300.

Hawkins, G. (1991) 'Reforming the Australia Council: the legacies and limitations of community arts', *Culture & Policy*, 3: 13–24.

Hesmondhalgh, D. and Baker, S. (2010) '"A very complicated version of freedom": conditions and experiences of creative labour in three cultural industries', *Poetics*, 38: 4–20.

Hesmondhalgh, D. and Saha, A. (2013) 'Race, ethnicity, and cultural production', *Popular Communication*, 11: 179–95.

Hesmondhalgh, D., Nisbett, M., Oakley, K. and Lee, D. (2015) 'Were New Labour's cultural policies neo-liberal?', *International Journal of Cultural Policy*, 21(1): 97–114.

Hickey-Moody, A.C. and Willcox, M. (2025) 'Feminist fabulation as "fighting back"', *Frontiers in Communication*, 10: 1542825.

Hickey-Moody, A., Cornell, C., Kelly, P., Hartley, S. and Ciaffaglione, A. (2025) 'Vital Arts: interim project report', RMIT University, [online], Available from: https://vital-arts.org/project-report-2025

Holcombe-James, I., Flore, J. and Hendry, N.A. (2022) 'Digital arts and culture in Australia: promissory discourses and uncertain realities in pandemic times', *Media International Australia*, 192(1): 115–29.

Holdsworth, C. (2018) 'Generic distinctiveness and the entrepreneurial self: a case study of English higher education', *Journal of Youth Studies*, 21(9): 1216–31.

hooks, b. (1989) *Talking Back: Thinking Feminist, Thinking Black*, South End Press.

Horton, J. and Pyer, M. (2017) 'Introduction: Children, young people and "care"', in J. Horton and M. Pyer (eds) *Children, Young People and Care*, Routledge, pp 1–25.

Howard, P.G. (2018) 'Twenty-first century learning as a radical re-thinking of education in the service of life', *Education Sciences*, 8(4): 189.

Howie, L. and Campbell, P. (2016) 'Guerrilla selfhood: imagining young people's entrepreneurial futures', *Journal of Youth Studies*, 19(7): 906–20.

Hrach, S. (2021) *Minding Bodies: How Physical Space, Sensation, and Movement Affect Learning*, West Virginia University Press.

Hunter, I. (1988) *Culture and Government: The Emergence of Literary Education*, Macmillan.

Hunter, I. (2020) *Rethinking the School: Subjectivity, Bureaucracy, Criticism*, Routledge.

Hunter, M.A. (1999) 'Redefining "industry": young people and cultural policy in Australia', *Media International Australia*, 90(1): 123–38.

Idriss, S. (2016) 'Racialisation in the creative industries and the Arab-Australian multicultural artist', *Journal of Intercultural Studies*, 37(4): 406–20.

Idriss, S., Butler, R. and Harris, A. (2022) 'Interrogating race, unsettling whiteness: concepts of transitions, enterprise and mobilities in Australian youth studies', *Journal of Youth Studies*, 25(9): 1251–67.

Ikonen, H.-M. and Nikunen, M. (2019) 'Young adults and the tuning of the entrepreneurial mindset in neoliberal capitalism', *Journal of Youth Studies*, 22(6): 824–38.

ILO (2022) 'Greater progress on diversity and inclusion essential to rebuild productive and resilient workplaces', ILO, Available from: https://www.ilo.org/global/about-the-ilo/newsroom/news/WCMS_841085/lang--en/index.htm

Ivinson, G.M. and Renold, E.J. (2022) 'Emplaced activism: what-if environmental education attuned to young people's entanglements with post-industrial landscapes?', *Australian Journal of Environmental Education*, 38(3–4): 415–30.

Jakobsson, M. (2016) 'Achievement', in H. Lowood and R. Guins (eds) *Debugging Game History: A Critical Lexicon*, MIT Press, pp 1–11.

Jha, S. (2023) 'Diversity and inclusion policies are at threat: here's how to keep them on track', WEF, [online] 13 September, Available from: https://www.weforum.org/stories/2023/09/diversity-and-inclusion-policies-are-at-threat-here-s-how-to-keep-them-on-track/

Jones, A. (2018) 'Vocational education for the twenty-first century', Centre for the Study of Higher Education, Melbourne University.

Jung, I. (2016) 'Introduction', in I. Jung, M. Nishimura and T. Sasao (eds) *Liberal Arts Education and Colleges in East Asia: Possibilities and Challenges in the Global Age*, Springer, pp 1–12.

Kelly, P. (2000) 'Youth as an artefact of expertise: problematizing the practice of youth studies in an age of uncertainty', *Journal of Youth Studies*, 3(3): 301–15.

Kelly, P. (2006) 'The entrepreneurial self and "youth at-risk": exploring the horizons of identity in the twenty-first century', *Journal of Youth Studies*, 9(1): 17–32.

Kelly, P. (2013) *The Self as Enterprise: Foucault and the Spirit of 21st-Century Capitalism*, Ashgate.

Kelly, P. and Harrison, L. (2009) *Working in Jamie's Kitchen: Salvation, Passion and Young Workers*, Palgrave.

Kelly, P. and Pike, J. (eds) (2017) *Neo-liberalism and Austerity: The Moral Economies of Young People's Health and Well-Being*, Palgrave Macmillan.

Kennedy, K.J., Pavlova, M. and Lee, J.C.K. (eds) (2022) *Soft Skills and Hard Values: Meeting Education's 21st-Century Challenges*, Routledge.

Khan, R. (2010) 'Going "mainstream": evaluating the instrumentalisation of multicultural arts', *International Journal of Cultural Policy*, 16(2): 184–99.

Khan, R. (2013) 'Rethinking cultural capital and community-based arts', *Journal of Sociology*, 49(2–3): 357–72.

Khan, R. (2020) 'Why we need to talk about race in the arts, or the limits of aspirational diversity', in T. Bennett, D. Stevenson, F. Myers and T. Winikoff (eds) *The Australian Art Field: Practices, Policies, Institutions*, Routledge, pp 158–69.

Kim, K.H., Cramond, B. and Vantassel-Baska, J. (2010) 'The relationship between creativity and intelligence', in J.C. Kaufman and R.J. Sternberg (eds) *The Cambridge Handbook of Creativity*, Cambridge University Press, pp 395–412.

Lamb, S., Jackson, J. and Rumberger, R. (2018) 'ISCY technical paper: measuring 21st-century skills in ISCY', Centre for International Research on Education Systems (International Study of City Youth).

Laughey, D. (2006) *Music and Youth Culture*, Edinburgh University Press.

Lawrence, S.E.L. (2022) 'The majority world: what's in a phase?', Philanthropy Australia, [online] 4 November, Available from: https://www.philanthropy.org.au/news-and-stories/the-majority-world-whats-in-a-phrase/

Lazzarato, M. (2012) *The Making of the Indebted Man: An Essay on the Neoliberal Condition*, Semiotext(e).

Lenette, C. (2019) *Arts-Based Methods in Refugee Research*, Springer.

Leonard, P. and Wilde, R. (2019) *Getting In and Getting On in the Youth Labour Market: Governing Young People's Employability in Regional Context*, Policy Press.

Livermore, D.A. (2009) *Leading with Cultural Intelligence: The Real Secret to Success*, American Management Association.

Lorde, A. (2012) *Sister Outsider: Essays and Speeches*, Crossing Press.

Lorey, I. (2015) *State of Insecurity: Government of the Precarious*, Verso.

MacDonald, R., Shildrick, T. and Blackman, S.J. (eds) (2010) *Young People, Class and Place*, Routledge.

Márquez, I., Lanzeni, D. and Masanet, M.J. (2023) 'Teenagers as curators: digitally mediated curation of the self on Instagram', *Journal of Youth Studies*, 26(7): 907–24.

Martuccelli, D. (2007) *Gramáticas del individuo*, Losada.

MCEETYA (2008) 'Melbourne declaration on educational goals for young Australians', MCEETYA.

McGillivray, D., McPherson, G., Jones, J. and McCandlish, A. (2016) 'Young people, digital media making and critical digital citizenship', *Leisure Studies*, 35(6): 724–38.

McGuigan, J. (2014) 'Creative labour, cultural work and individualisation', in C. Bilton (ed) *Creativity and Cultural Policy*, Routledge, pp 93–105.

McLaughlin, J. (2024) 'Bringing disability studies and youth studies together to enhance understandings of youth transitions', *Journal of Youth Studies*, 27(6): 904–19.

McLeod, J. and Wright, K. (2016) 'What does wellbeing do? An approach to defamiliarize keywords in youth studies', *Journal of Youth Studies*, 19(6): 776–92.

McRobbie, A. (2002) 'From Holloway to Hollywood: happiness at work in the new cultural economy?', in P. DuGay and M. Pryke (eds) *Cultural Economy: Cultural Analysis and Commercial Life*, SAGE, pp 97–114.

McRobbie, A. (2016) *Be Creative: Making a Living in the New Culture Industries*, Polity.

Meaney, M. (2020) 'Kids! Broadway, rock and roll, and the younger generation', master's thesis, State University of New York at Binghamton.

Mearns, H. (1925) *Creative Youth: How a School Environment Set Free the Creative Spirit*, Doubleday.

Mearns, H. (1940/41) *Creative Adult: Self-Education in the Art of Living*, Doubleday.

Media Diversity Australia (2022) 'Australian television news is far more Anglo-Celtic than the country it covers: lack of diversity led from the top', Media Diversity Australia, [online] 17 August, Available from: https://www.mediadiversityaustralia.org/wp-content/uploads/2020/08/Press-release_final.pdf

Meredyth, D. (1991) 'Personality and personnel: rationalities for the humanities', in I. Hunter, D. Meredyth, B. Smith and G.S. Nathan (eds) *Accounting for the Humanities: The Language of Culture and the Logic of Government*, Institute for Cultural Policy Studies, Griffith University, pp 117–89.

Moje, E.B. (2002) 'Re-framing adolescent literacy research for new times: studying youth as a resource', *Literacy Research and Instruction*, 41(3): 211–28.

Montgomery, D. (2017) 'The rise of creative youth development', *Arts Education Policy Review*, 118(1): 1–18.

Moore, B. (2004) *The Australian Oxford Dictionary* (2nd edn), Oxford University Press.

Morgan, G., Wood, J. and Nelligan, P. (2013) 'Beyond the vocational fragments: creative work, precarious labour and the idea of "flexploitation"', *The Economic and Labour Relations Review*, 24(3): 397–415.

Morgan, G. and Nelligan, P. (2018) *The Creativity Hoax: Precarious Work in the Gig Economy*, Anthem Press.

Mouritsen, J. and Kreiner, K. (2016) 'Accounting, decisions and promises', *Accounting, Organizations and Society*, 49: 21–31.

Mozilla Foundation and Peer 2 Peer University (2012) 'Open badges for lifelong learning', Available from: https://wiki.mozilla.org/images/5/59/OpenBadges-Working-Paper_012312.pdf

Neff, G., Wissinger, E. and Zukin, S. (2005) 'Entrepreneurial labor among cultural producers: "cool" jobs in "hot" industries', *Social Semiotics*, 15(3): 307–34.

Noonan, M. and Kelly, P. (2019) 'Young people and the gendered and aesthetic dimensions of enterprise: stories from a "rust belt" city', *Journal of Youth Studies*, 23(4): 481–98.

Nussbaum, M.C. (2000) *Women and Human Development: The Capabilities Approach* (The Seeley Lectures 3), Cambridge University Press.

Oakley, K. and O'Connor, J. (eds) (2015) *Class and Exclusion at Work: The Case of UK Film and Television*, Routledge.

OECD (2020) 'Youth and COVID-19: response, recovery and resilience', OECD.

Oinonen, E. (2018) 'Under pressure to become: from a student to entrepreneurial self', *Journal of Youth Studies*, 21(10): 1344–60.

Osterman, P., Lowe, N., Anderson, B., Trotter, J., Iskander, N. and Agarwala, R. (2022) 'A forum on the politics of skills', *ILR Review*, 75(5): 1348–68.

Patterson, A. (1993) '"Personal response" and English teaching', in D. Meredyth and D. Tyler (eds) *Child and Citizen: Genealogies of Schooling and Subjectivity*, Institute for Cultural Policy Studies, pp 61–86.

Petersen, A. (2018) 'Capitalising on ageing anxieties: promissory discourse and the creation of an "anti-ageing treatment" market', *Journal of Sociology*, 54(2): 191–202.

Phoenix, A. and Pattynama, P. (2006) 'Intersectionality', *European Journal of Women's Studies*, 13(3): 187–92.

Redmalm, D. and Skoglund, A. (2020) 'Rethinking government and its economy with Giorgio Agamben: the *homo sacer* in alternative entrepreneurship', *The Sociological Review*, 68(5): 948–64.

Ringrose, J., Milne, B., Horeck, T. and Mendes, K. (2024) 'Postdigital bodies: young people's experiences of algorithmic, tech-facilitated body shaming and image-based sexual abuse during and after the COVID-19 pandemic in England', *Youth*, 4(3): 1058–75.

Rizvi, F. and Choo, S.S. (2020) 'Education and cosmopolitanism in Asia: an introduction', *Asia Pacific Journal of Education*, 40(1): 1–9.

Robinson, B.A. and Schmitz, R.M. (2021) 'Beyond resilience: resistance in the lives of LGBTQ youth', *Sociology Compass*, 15(12): e12947.

Robinson, K. and Aronica L. (2009) *The Element*, Penguin.

Rodó-de-Zárate, M. (2017) 'Who else are they? Conceptualizing intersectionality for childhood and youth research', *Children's Geographies*, 15(1): 23–35.

Salamanca, N. (2023) 'Financial pressures are seen widely as the key barrier to getting a university education', in 'Taking the pulse of the nation: informing Australian economic and social policy', University of Melbourne and Roy Morgan-Melbourne Institute, Available from: https://roymorgan-cms-prod.s3.ap-southeast-2.amazonaws.com/wp-content/uploads/2023/11/01052931/9327-MI-RM-TTPN-27-October-2023-015.pdf

Sayer, A. (2000) 'Moral economy and political economy', *Studies in Political Economy*, 61(1): 79–103.

Serrano, A. and Martín, P. (2017) 'From "employab-ility" to "entrepreneurial-ity" in Spain: youth in the spotlight in times of crisis', *Journal of Youth Studies*, 20(7): 798–821.

Shliakhovchuk, E. (2021) 'After cultural literacy: new models of intercultural competency for life and work in a VUCA world', *Educational Review*, 73(2): 229–50.

Smith, B. (1991) 'Crime and the classics: the humanities and government in the nineteenth century Australian university', in I. Hunter, D. Meredyth, B. Smith and G.S. Nathan (eds) *Accounting for the Humanities: The Language of Culture and the Logic of Government*, Institute for Cultural Policy Studies, Griffith University, pp 67–115.

Stow, D. (1850) *The Training System, the Moral Training School, and the Normal Seminary* (8th edn), Longman, Brown, Green and Longmans.

Stringer, E.T. (2014) *Action Research* (4th edn), SAGE.

Thomas, K. (ed) (1999) *The Oxford Book of Work*, Oxford University Press.

Thorndike, E.L. (1898) 'Animal intelligence: an experimental study of the associative processes in animals', *The Psychological Review: Monograph Supplements*, 2(4): i–109.

Threadgold, S., Farrugia, D. and Coffey, J. (2021) 'Challenging the structure/agency binary: youthful culture, labour and embodiments', in M. Nico and A. Caetano (eds) *Structure and Agency in Young People's Lives*, Routledge, pp 13–29.

Thrift, N. (2005) *Knowing Capitalism*, SAGE.

Throsby, D. and Petetskaya, K. (2017) 'Making art work: an economic study of professional artists in Australia', Australia Council for the Arts.

Thrower, J. (2024) 'University is expensive: impacts of rising university costs on young people', The Australia Institute.

Trinca, H. and Fox, C. (2004) *Better than Sex: How a Whole Generation Got Hooked on Work*, Random House.

van Laar, E., van Deursen, A., van Dijk, J. and Haan, J. (2020) 'Determinants of 21st-century skills and 21st-century digital skills for workers: a systematic literature review', *Sage Open*, 10(1): 1–14.

Uboldi, A. (2024) 'Everything is in My Hands. Creative Subjectivities in Privileged Arts School Students', *Cultural Sociology*, 18(3): 370-88.

Virno, P. (2001/4) *A Grammar of the Multitude*, Semiotext(e).

von Benzon, N. and Wilkinson, C. (2019) *Intersectionality and Difference in Childhood and Youth*, Routledge.

Vromen, A. (2008) 'Building virtual spaces: young people, participation and the internet', *Australian Political Studies Association*, 43(1): 79–97.

Walsh, L. and Black, R. (2020) '"Flexible ongoing": the young university student as homo promptus', *Journal of Youth Studies*, 24(4): 499–514.

Warren, A., and Gibson, C. (2017) 'Subcultural enterprises, brand value, and limits to financialized growth: the rise and fall of corporate surfing brands', *Geoforum*, 87: 177–87.

Warren, C., Batra, R., Loureiro, S. and Bagozzi, R. (2019) 'Brand coolness', *Journal of Marketing*, 83(5): 36–56.

WEF (2015) 'New vision for education: unlocking the potential of technology', WEF, [online], Available from: https://widgets.weforum.org/nve-2015/chapter1.html

WEF (2016) 'New vision for education: fostering social and emotional learning through technology', WEF, Available from: http://www3.weforum.org/docs/WEF_New_Vision_for_Education.pdf

Westbury, M. (2006) 'Once a professional token youth', *Griffith Review*, 13.

Wheelahan, L. and Moodie, G. (2022) 'Gig qualifications for the gig economy: micro-credentials and the "hungry mile"', *Higher Education*, 83(6): 1279–95.

Wilde, O. (1891) *The Soul of Man Under Socialism*. Fortnightly Review.

Williams, R. (1961) *The Long Revolution*, Columbia University Press.

Wyn, J., Khan, R. and Dadvand, B. (2018) 'Multicultural Youth Australia census status report 2017/2018', Melbourne Graduate School of Education, University of Melbourne, Available from: https://cmy.wpenginepowered.com/wp-content/uploads/2019/11/MY-Australia-Census-Status-Report-2017-18.pdf

Index

A

achievement, subjects of 51
action research 94–5
Action Research Industry Group 80
Adams, C.N. 108
adaptability 89, 106, 138, 144, 157, 158, 160
aesthetic scrutiny, of work 45, 47, 48
agency *see* youth agency
All-Ages Tour 109–11
Animal Intelligence (Thorndike) 26
'art for art's sake' 90
aspirational diversity 119
aspirations 64, 114, 148
  classed 51–2, 146–7
  micro-credentials and 140, 144–8
  possibilities and 161–2, 163, 165
  youth agency and 139, 151
Australian Centre for the Moving Image (ACMI) 84
Australian Research Council (ARC), Linkage Project Scheme 79, 81, 82
Australian Theatre for Young People (ATYP) 4, 79, 94, 100–6, 149, 157–8, 163

B

Bacchi, C. 145
badges *see* digital badges
Bauman, Zygmunt 44, 45–7, 48, 49
Beck, Ulrich 45
Biesta, G.J. 63
Big hART 5
biological and social age, difference between 28
Black Lives Matter 121
Blackmore, Jill 59
Bloom's taxonomy 91–3, 96, 97
Borup, M. 77
Bourdieu, Pierre 28–9
Brave New World of Work (Beck) 45

C

capabilities *see* 21st-century skills
Carclew 88, 149–50, 154, 158–9, 163
careers 11, 22, 23, 52, 113, 114, 149, 162
Centre for Multicultural Youth (CMY) 79, 94, 122–3
  Culture Spring programme *see* Culture Spring programme (CMY)
  MY Education programme 123
character qualities 38, 59, 89, 90, 95, 106, 116
Choo, S.S. 116
citizenship 121
  global citizenship education 116–17
  informed 62
  organisational 113
  value-based 115–16
civic engagement 5

class privilege 10
CLOCK Your Skills 2, 12–13, 79–80
Clockwork Orange, A: A Play with Music 103–6
CMY *see* Centre for Multicultural Youth (CMY)
Coalition government 80, 81
code of conduct 52
cognitive competencies 60, 95, 111
collaborative skills 55, 57, 61, 84, 89, 95, 105–6, 144, 149
communication skills 4, 105, 106, 117, 163
confidence 4, 62, 98, 99, 110, 146, 147, 151, 157, 158, 160, 163
conscientiousness 61
consumer culture 3, 46–9, 141
consumerism 46–7, 141
Contact Theatre, UK 4
Cook, J. 37
cool jobs 119, 146, 161–2, 165
coordination 97, 104, 105, 106, 110
Corfield, Fraser 5, 83–4, 85–6
Corrugated Iron Youth Arts 4, 5, 84, 86
costs of living, impact of 22
COVID-19 pandemic 1, 37–8
creative art practices *see* practices
Creative Australia 72–3, 79, 80, 81–2
creative education 23–7, 33
'Creative nation' (document) 81
Creative Partnerships Australia 82
creative writing 25, 26–7, 137
critical thinking 4, 59, 84, 89, 91, 95, 99, 106, 109, 116, 136
Csikszentmihalyi, Mihaly 98
cultural circuits of capitalism 53
cultural complexity and volatility 118
cultural intelligence (CQ) 112, 117
cultural policies 78, 81–2, 119, 138, 148
culture 50, 115–18
  awareness of 88, 89, 106, 113, 115, 116, 117
  competence 127, 150
  literacy 115, 117, 118, 135
  marketisation of *see* Culture Spring programme (CMY)
Culture Spring programme (CMY) 122–3
  Black feminist and intersectional theory and 126–32
  cultural knowledge and its value 133–5
  intersectionality and 127
  marketing, packaging and value proposition 124–5
  power asymmetries 132–3
  structure, positioning and messaging 124
curiosity 6, 89, 106

D

Deakin University 79
Deleuze, Gilles 50
Descartes, René 97
Dewey, John 25–6
digital badges 67–73, 145, 146, 147
  Open Badges project of the Mozilla Foundation 77
  open-source 7, 73
  problem space of 73–6
  see also micro-credentials
digital spaces 7–10, 11
discipline 26, 103, 120, 137, 139, 141, 142, 143, 147, 157, 158
diversity cred 112–15
Duncan, Kate 110
duty 48
Duxbury, L. 96

E

educational privilege 10
Element, The (Robinson and Aronica) 99–100
embodiment, arts and 96–9, 104
empowerment 11, 16, 73, 108, 122, 124, 147, 148, 150, 159

enterprise and entrepreneurship 51–6, 121, 151
entrepreneurialism 54, 56, 119–20, 151
ethics 33, 47, 48, 61
  ethical selfhood 138
  ethical surveillance 23–7, 140
  post-Fordist manifestations 51–2
European Commission (EC), entrepreneurship promotion 54–5
Evely, Christine 84–5, 107, 108
existential problems 21–2
expectations 72, 76–7, 134, 143

F

facilitators of arts
  positionalities of 108–9
  and young people, mutual respect between 4
Farrugia, David 49, 50–2
feedback process 83–4
fetishisation of skills 38, 44, 63
fieldworks 99–100
  ACMI and Film It 106–9
  ATYP 100–6
  Push and FReeZA All-Ages Tour 109–11
  see also partnerships
Film It programme 106–9
Flew, Terry 151
flexploitation 119
flow state 98
Foundation for Young Australians (FYA) 54, 55–6
foundational literacies 38, 89
foundational skills 95, 98–9
FReeZA programme 109–11
Future Foundations 79, 150–1, 154–5, 159–60, 163
future of work 36, 38, 51, 53, 108, 144, 147, 148
  reimagine 139–40, 152, 160
  skills demanded for 2
  see also work

G

Geelong, Victoria 36
generative futures 165
generative potentials
  of partnerships 152, 154–5
  of practice 160
Gill, Rosalind 122
global citizenship education 116
global crises 22, 138, 164
Global Entrepreneurship Monitor (GEM) 53
global grammars of enterprise 51, 53–6, 64
globalisation 3, 36, 44, 53, 116, 161
governance of youth 17, 33, 108–9, 124, 134, 137–40, 142–3, 151, 160, 161
  creative education and 21–7
  partnerships and 152–6
  post-governance critiques 142–4
  skills discourse and 144–8
government partnerships 78
governmental intervention, youth arts and media as 29–34
Greater London Council 31
Guattari, Felix 50

H

Hardt, Michael 50
Hawkins, Gay 29, 148
Hickey-Moody, Anna 143
Hrach, Susan 97
Hunter, Ian 24–5, 140

I

immaterial goods 50
inclusion 5, 16, 112, 113, 115, 121–2, 125, 132, 149
individuals, and consumerism 46
industries and cultures, of youth arts 3–6
informal education 3–6, 7–8, 11, 73–7, 86
initiatives 57, 89, 106
innovation-based economy, skills requirements in 90–3

intellectual openness 60
intercultural dialogue 5
intercultural literacy 117
intercultural understanding 116
International Labour Organization (ILO) 112
international mindedness 116
inter-personal competencies 61
intersectionality 13–17
intra-personal competencies 60–1

J

Jakobsson, M. 74
job satisfaction and fulfilment *see* work
Jones, Anne 57

K

knowledge 60

L

Labor government 80, 81, 82
Lamb, Stephen 57–8, 59
leadership 61, 106, 159–60
lifelong learning 63, 73, 74, 89
LOUD festival 32–3, 142, 150, 164

M

manual labour, and dignity 43–4
market capture, of justice work 132–3
material problems 21–2
McQuire, Scott 143
Mearns, Hughes 26–7
media 142
  ACMI Film It and 107
  creative industries case study 128–132
  digital 7–8
  as governmental intervention 29–34
  Mozilla open badges and 73
'Melbourne declaration on educational goals for young Australians' (MCEETYA) 62
mental health challenges 23
micro-credentials 3, 7, 8, 86–7, 145–7
  accessibility 11
  barriers 12–13
  digital 72, 77
  feedback process 83–4
  justifying parents and families 85
  potential to redefine education 84–5
  practice and skills 89–90
  promissory partnership 83–6
  reflection and 84
  skills development and 120
  see also digital badges
Microsoft 74
middle-class manners 50
mind–body dualism 96–9
mindfulness 96–9
modernisation 44
modernity 28–9
moral development, in school system 24, 137, 140
moral judgements 49
moral value 48
Morgan, George 63
Mozilla 73, 76, 77
mutual respect, between facilitators and young people 4

N

National Programme for Excellence in the Arts, Australia 80
National University of Singapore 79
Negri, Antonio 50
Nelligan, Pariece 63
neoliberal 148, 151, 153
  capitalism 51
  enterprise, selfhood and 52–3
  globalisation 36
  individualism 160, 163
  instrumentalism 72, 78
  responsibilisation 145, 155
neurodivergent learners 91, 93
NGV Ambassadors programme 150, 154, 159, 163

Nhat Hanh, Thich 97
'Nozin' around' (skit) 29–30, 142

O

Octapod (Marcus Westbury) 139, 142, 164
Open Badges project of the Mozilla Foundation 77
outcomes, of youth arts programmes 4

P

partnerships 78–9, 152–3
  fieldworks *see* fieldworks
  generative potentials 154–5
  in policy discourse 152–3
  promissory 83–6
  risk sharing and responsibilisation 153
  as sites of contestation 155–6
  tensions and negotiations 153–4
  Vital Arts and 79–82
passion, subjects of 51
Peer 2 Peer Foundation 73, 77
peer-to-peer learning 6, 75, 150
persistence/grit 89, 106, 115
play, seeing activities as 6, 85
pleasurable experience, work as 47
policies
  cultural 78, 81–2, 119, 138, 148
  discourse, in partnerships 152–3
  EU entrepreneurship 55
  multicultural 119
  problematisation of youth 16–17, 21
possibilities 161
  cool jobs 161–2
  double life of 163–4
  equitable 164–5
  unequal 162
  as world making 164
  youth programmes and 163
post-governance techniques 142–3
post-secondary education, cost of 22–3
practices 156–60
  defined 95–6
  generative potentials of 160
  importance of 160–1
  of leadership 106, 159–60
  21st-century skills and 89–90
  see also fieldworks
precarious labour 44, 52, 118–19
problem of young people
  history for 35–8
  in micro-cred economy 147
  re-imaging and re-making 137–44
problem solving abilities 59, 89, 90, 91, 99, 104, 106, 109
productive energy, creativity as 63
progressive education 25–6, 77
project-based learning 11, 77
promissory discourses 72, 76, 77, 83–6, 87
public education 23–4, 25, 29, 140
Push Youth Music Organisation, The 79, 109–11, 150, 158

R

race 117–22
racialised young people 112–15
RANT Arts 5
reflection, and micro-credentials 84
refugee communities, programmes in 5, 122–3
research
  action research 94–5
  young people in 27–9, 138
  in youth arts settings 93–5
responsibilisation 145, 153, 155, 160
'Revive' (document) 82
risk society 45
Rizvi, F. 116
RMIT University 79
Robinson, B.A. 99–100

S

school designs 24
Scrogings, Zoe 84, 86
self
  as an enterprise 48, 49
  formation of 45

self-evaluation, positive core 61
selfhood management 140–1
service industries 50
sexualised aspects of performance 50
Shliakhovchuk, E. 117
skills, as state of becoming 2
see also 21st-century skills
social awareness 106
social inclusion *see* inclusion
social life 59, 63, 90, 111
Stow, David 24
strategic essentialism 121
Stringer, Ernest T. 94
subcultural credibility 120–1
symbolic activity, materialisation of 77

T

Taxonomy of educational objectives (Bloom) 91–3, 96, 97
teamwork *see* collaborative skills; partnerships
technology futures 76–8
Thorndike, Edward L. 26
Thrift, Nigel 53
traditional degrees vs micro-credentials 67–70
traditional schooling 4–5, 8, 10–11
21st-century skills 38, 56–63, 144–8
creative practices and 89–90
culture and 115–18

V

Vital Arts: Skilling Young People for their Futures (research project) 2, 11–13, 64, 78
intersectionality approach 16
and partnerships 79–82
vocation as privilege 48
vocational education 57

W

WEF *see* World Economic Forum (WEF)
Westbury, Marcus 31–3, 147, 150, 164
see also Octapod (Marcus Westbury)
Westmore, Garry 108
Wilde, Oscar 43–4
wildness of youth 6–12, 142–3
work
ethic *see* ethics
evaluation of 47
as the meaning of life, 6, 21, 38, 44–5, 46–7, 48, 140
of performance, and ATYP 100–6, 149, 157–8, 163
as self-fulfilment 44–7, 48
society, beyond 39–51
see also future of work
work society
mobilising embodied affect to negotiate employment 49–50
promises of 44–5
World Economic Forum (WEF) 58–9, 89, 90

Y

Young Ones, The 29–31, 139, 142
youth agency 6–12, 147–8
intersectionality 16
reframing 33–4
youth governance *see* governance of youth
Youth Theatre Ireland 4
youth transitions 114, 138
youth unemployment 29, 31–3, 36, 52, 141, 164